DR. MARILOU RYDER
JESSICA THOMPSON

Don't Forget Your Sweater, Girl

SISTER to SISTER SECRETS FOR AGING WITH PURPOSE AND HUMOR

DON'T FORGET YOUR SWEATER, GIRL

Sister to Sister Secrets for Aging with Purpose and Humor

ISBN: 978-0-9904103-3-1

Library of Congress Control Number: 2019902512

understanding that the publisher is not engaged in rendering legal, medical, or professional advice. Although the author and publisher have made every effort to ensure that the information in this book was correct at press time, the author and publisher do not assume and hereby disclaim any liability to any party for any loss, damage, or disruption caused by errors or omissions, whether such errors or omissions result from negligence, accident, or any other cause. Neither the Publisher nor Authors shall be liable for damages arising from the information within this book. The fact that an organization or website is referred to in this work as a citation and/or potential source of future information does not mean that the Authors or Publisher endorse the information, the organization or website may provide or recommendations it may make. Further, readers should be aware that internet websites listed in this work may have changed or disappeared since this work was written and when it was read. All names and identifying details of interviewees for this book have been changed to protect the privacy of individuals.

Publicity Rights

For information on publicity, author interviews, presentation, or subsidiary rights, contact:

Dr. Marilou Ryder: drmlr@yahoo.com 760-900-0556

Jessica Thompson: rthompson22@comcast.net 978-879-9288

Back cover photo: ©Del Ryder

Book design by StoriesToTellBooks.com

Printed in the United States of America

Delmar Publishing, Huntington Beach, CA 92648

Does this one come in Pink?

How about Green?

Books by Dr. Marilou Ryder

Rules of the Game: How to Win a Job in Educational Leadership
Delmar Publishing, 2016

*92 Tips from the Trenches: How to Stay in the Game as an
Educational Leader*
Delmar Publishing, 2014

*The SeXX Factor: Breaking the Unwritten Codes that Sabotage
Personal and Professional Lives*
New Horizon Press, 2003

Other Publications by Dr. Marilou Ryder

Preparing for Your Next Leadership Position
Leadership, March/April 2016

Leadership Begins at the End of Your Comfort Zone
Leadership March/April 2013

Go to the Head of the Class
The School Administrator, October 2009

Superintendent Gets Taken for a Ride
The School Administrator, February 2009

Cultivating Women Leaders through a Network
The School Administrator, November 2008

Create Your Own Aspiring Administrators Symposium
Leadership Magazine, 2006

Moving on Up: Promoting At Risk Students
Leadership Magazine, 2002

*The Impact of Male Gender Dissonance on Women's Potential
Eligibility for Advancement to the Position of Superintendent*
UNI Dissertation Services, 1999

Women in Educational Leadership: Breaking the Norm
Thrust for Educational Leadership May/June 1994

MEET THE AUTHOR

Dr. Marilou Ryder

Age	70
Childhood Ambition	To become a veterinarian
Best Health Tip	Omega Fish Oil
Inspiration	Powerful women
Best Money Saver	Happy-Hours
Personal Quote	"Be audacious"
Defining Moment	Becoming a superintendent
Biggest Challenge	Becoming a superintendent
Favorite Song	Sounds of Silence
Greatest Success	Raising my son to become a good person
Best Make-up Tip	Using Retin-A daily
What I learned from writing this book	Pick up my feet when walking and live the good life while I still can!

MEET THE AUTHOR

Jessica Thompson

Age	61
Childhood Ambition	To become a fashion designer
Best Health Tip	Aquaphor
Inspiration	My daughters
Best Money Saver	Carrying my own golf bag
Personal Quote	"You got this!"
Defining Moment	First child graduating from college
Biggest Challenge	Running my first 5K at 55
Favorite Song	Landslide
Greatest Success	Seeing my daughters on their own
Best Make-up Tip	Volumize L'Oréal Mascara
What I learned from writing this book	Exercise my mind just as much as my body to keep strong and healthy and in the moment!

Contents

INTRODUCTIONS   xiii

Old Age is Not a Noun   xiii

Tie It Up in a Pink Bow   xix

Why You Should Read This Book   1

Show Me the Stats!   7

Living the Good Life!   19

UP CLOSE AND PERSONAL

Liz, Age 67   25

Sandy, Age 68   37

Susan, Age 69   53

Shelly, Age 72   63

Anna, Age 73   79

Barb, Age 73   95

Irene, Age 81   107

June, Age 88   123

Rose, Age 88   137

Mary Beth, Age 91   151

Fannie and Gwen, Ages 100   165

FINAL IMPRESSIONS   189

Ok Ladies. You know the rules... mouth guards in at all times. Goggles on at all time and no high sticks. I'm adding a new rule for today's game. Run as SLOW as you can so I can keep up with all of you. Oh yeah, and if I hear any of you call me an old lady you will get a red card and be on the bench.

Let's play Ball!

ACKNOWLEDGEMENTS

*D*on't *Forget Your Sweater* has been an ongoing project over a four-year span. What began as an initial online questionnaire eventually morphed into face-to-face interviews, phone conferences and individual written narratives from women on both US coasts. The advice and stories in this publication would not have been possible without the endless hours of time donated by women who agreed to be interviewed in a variety of ways throughout the life of this project. We extend our appreciation and thanks to the many women ages 60-100 who shared their stories, suggestions and advice to other women as they prepare to enter their own decades of senior living. The women represented in this book came from many different walks of life. The field of women who shared their stories transverse a wide spectrum which included racial, gender, social, and economic diversity. The process involved interviewing all participants and was modeled after a qualitative research design methodology. As a result all women included in this project asked that confidentially and anonymity be provided for them to allow for spontaneity and complete honesty. Despite my background as a qualitative researcher, I felt that using identifiers such as 'Interviewee 1' would be too impersonal. Our strategy for using names as identifiers involved asking our participants to choose their own pseudonym, which also provided a great way to help build rapport during the interviews.

Dr. Marilou Ryder

Professor Doctoral Studies

DON'T FORGET YOUR SWEATER, GIRL

As a child I remember my mother always nagging me to bring my sweater or jacket whenever I left the house. Or if out in public she would say, "Put your sweater on, don't you think I know when you're cold?" More often than not I would leave it somewhere in my travels and have to confess days later that my pink sweater was either hanging over some boxes in Bobby Roser's garage or left somewhere on the school bus. Unfortunately, as a mother myself I would repeat that mantra for my own kid but since I am a Type A obsessive personality I always knew where that sweater got left. Now approaching 70 years old I don't leave home without it… my sweater that is. You never know when you'll end up sitting in a cold restaurant, movie theater or just plain spike a cold spell all of your own. To be quite honest, ever since turning 68 I'm cold most of the time, even though I live in California. The worst part of having to remember to bring a sweater with me whenever I leave the house is to leave it behind. Too often, I take my sweater off, especially if seated at a restaurant in the sun, and hang it on the back of my chair because now, "I'm too hot!" Then one glass of wine and it's all over. My sweater is left behind, not to be remembered for days. As a result of losing too many sweaters over the years my husband came up with a new slogan for our toolbox. It's called LOOK BACK. Whenever we are stationary, even for just a second and especially if seated, we pledge to say to one another, "Look Back" and invariably we spot sunglasses, jackets, iPhones, AND sweaters.

Marilou (70)

INTRODUCTIONS

OLD AGE IS NOT A NOUN

by Marilou Ryder (on the West Coast) Age 70

I plan to live forever. So far so good.
~Stephen Wright

Old age is not always a pretty sight and as we know can come without warning. When I turned 65 and then 66 in the blink of an eye, I found myself concentrating on "getting old". Pesky, nagging questions often woke me up from a deep sleep in the middle of the night. Who will take care of me in old age? How will I manage the finances if I get dementia? Why does everything suddenly hurt? Why can't I run that mile anymore? Why is my hair thinning?

I became absorbed listening in on conversations in which women would make references about getting old. Throughout my own daily interactions with people I would catch myself saying, *"I'm getting old... Gee my back hurts... That's what old age does to you..."* or my personal favorite...*"Getting old is not for sissies."* One day, a dear friend pulled me aside and cautioned me to tone it down with my 'old age' innuendoes. "If you continue with this *aging theme*," she warned, "people will begin to marginalize you and think you can't do your job. They will perceive you are too old to be in the workplace and start thinking about making room for a younger person. Your subtle 'aging' references," she warned, "may cause those 'upstairs' to consider you a has-been... and you know how that goes."

Her admonishment was the best advice ever received. How right she was... herself approaching 78 with a large role in an organization; a director of a large transportation company. This woman would put in demanding hours on a project and never blink an eye nor would she make an excuse for an oversight or mistake to 'being old'. She was, in my humble opinion, the poster child for 'senior citizens' in the workplace.

It didn't take long to up my game and change my behavior. Right away I eliminated conversational references alluding to "senior moments, getting old, or something hurts." After all, why would I blame aging, a natural phenomenon of life for why things weren't going well? Why would I reference aging as a handicap or something to whine about?

In retrospect, my life has never been about blaming. I've always put blamers in the victimization column... blaming others for things not going right in their lives. As an offshoot of this major life philosophy, I devoted the major part of my adult life studying and researching women; specifically, women in leadership. Throughout my studies I attempted to discover why it has been so difficult for women to gain access to top leadership positions. As a result of my research and doctoral thesis I wrote *The SeXX Factor: Breaking the Unwritten Codes that Sabotage Personal and Professional Lives,* a compelling research story that expressed a broader understanding of the barriers and obstacles that prevent women from succeeding in their careers. I love researching a problem... I love trying to find out how to dissect a problem and find solutions to make things better. I especially enjoy discovering strategies to help women succeed in a complicated, male dominated leadership world. Throughout my research, I never succumbed to blaming men for women's lack of leadership opportunities. Rather, I worked to find solutions for women to level the playing field.

So when it took me forever to land that top position of leadership in my field of education, the superintendency, I did not submit to excusatory tactics to make me feel better. I didn't go around saying, "I didn't get that job because I was a woman... it's just not fair!" Rather I thought of myself as men's equal and did what needed to be done to compete in that world. It should be noted, however, the task was a little more difficult than I envisioned. Six grueling job searches later, I finally secured a school superintendent position joining the ranks of 28% of women nationally who hold that leadership role. This was indeed a milestone for me personally and professionally. However, the discrepancy between men and women gaining equal access to this top educational leadership role still begs the question: why is it that 72% of school superintendents are men, when over 80% of America's public school teachers are women?

Thinking back on how hard I worked to gain access to a role statistically held by men and not get caught up in the blame game, I asked myself why would I start making excuses for growing old or for the lack of a better term, *becoming a Senior Citizen?* No way; I'd seen the light from my good friend. I knew I needed to take my love for research one step further. I would reach out to women in their later years of life and seek answers to how they manage to maintain their health, beauty, livelihood, security, and take a peek into their lives to examine how they perceive their world. We all know there are many books on the shelf about this very topic of getting old; it would be easy for me to buy one and be done with it. Thinking back on one of my favorite authors, Austin Kleon, (*Steal like an Artist*) I recalled one of his quotes that has always resonated with me; *"Write the book you want to read."* Great idea! Yes, I will write the book I want to read and I will share this book with other women. And it will be a great book, full of advice and positive strategies for women about living a good life with no blaming. And so the writing began. As luck would have it, I found a partner in crime to work with me on this project-my younger sister.

This book is a labor of love between two sisters. She and I are both aging, entering the second half of our lives. We are both curious and eager to learn more about how to navigate this period of aging. She lives on the East Coast near Boston and I live on the West Coast in Sunny

What to do when all your favorite NETFLIX men take a six month vacation.

California. Together we decided to take on this project to interview and survey women 60 years and older in the hope they would share their stories of growing old. And indeed they did… they offered advice on how they manage to thrive in this phase of their life rather than to merely survive. They shared their hopes and dreams for the present and future. They told us what makes them happy, how they navigate the side effects of aging, the phenomenon of loss and more importantly, the gains that old age brings. They shared their secrets for saving money, making friends, and staying active and presented wise suggestions for other women also trying to reach for the stars in their senior years. The women interviewed were candid and heartfelt and were incredibly gracious to be part of this project. For that, we are forever grateful for their generous donation of spirit, truth, and time.

What began as a lesson from my friend in how to escape the stereotypical effects of aging in the workplace transitioned into a wonderful, almost spiritual journey shared with women in the same space of life. No words can describe the gratitude expressed to these women who have become part of my world and a primary reason why my life as a senior woman continues to be positive, productive and engaging.

When you can't remember where you hid your online password list and have only 45 minutes left to shop on AMAZON PRIME DAY!

TIE IT UP IN A PINK BOW

by Jessica Thompson (on the East Coast) Age 61

Anything is possible with sunshine and a little pink.
~Lilly Pulitzer

There was something about entering my 60s I wasn't ready to accept. I felt the same, looked the same and lived my life the same as I had in my 50s. Having that number 60 attached to my being gave me the feeling I was different. Perhaps it was the thought I may have only 10 more healthy years left of my life. I wasn't ready to be old.

After the first year living with the number 60 I began to ease into this decade. I began to think about each of my days and how I could get the most out of each one. I began to respect each minute of each day and view them as a gift. As a family, when we lived on the Annisquam River we would experience the most amazing sunsets. When I knew one was on its way I would ask my daughters to stop whatever they were doing and watch the show. I would tell them to *cherish the moment.* I would be sure to tell them there would never be another one the same as the one they were seeing at this moment. Each sunset is special and was only there for a speck in time. I warned them… *treat these sunsets like each of your days and make each one special.* Each sunset you see will always be different and more beautiful than before.

Today we still have magnificent sunsets however we are no longer on the river; these sunsets are as elegant as ever. If our girls happen to visit I remind them to stop and cherish the moment. I think I made an impact on them because they are always texting me beautiful sunsets that warm my heart. This is how I view my life now. Each day is like a sunset filled with beautiful colors and shapes but only lasts a minute in time. So like my senior days they too only last a short time.

So now the challenge begins… I try to fill each day with as much joy as possible. I look at each day of my life as a package tied up in a beautiful pink bow. In each of my packages I put as many of the things in life I enjoy as possible. Of course, each package can't have everything I love in them, however I attempt to fill each one with healthy, happy and safe activities.

Some of my favorite activities are the sports of running and golf. At 61 I can still shoot in the 80s and on a great day hit my drives 180 yards. I try to run 3-4 miles a minimum of three days a week while listening to my 70s light rock Pandora station. Love the Eagles!

The moment I entered my next decade I learned how to play Mahjong and bridge. This is the only time I sit down during the day! My gardens are very special to me! I love to nurture their growth and enjoy their beauty. I'm forever working a part-time retail job here and there. One of my favorites was in a local family candy store. Oh yes… and I love doing needlepoint. My daughters tell me of all their possessions my needlepoint pillows are their favorites.

I love a good page turning book and a fast-moving mini-series on television. My husband tells me I'm a good cook and I think I would have to agree with him. I love to cook especially on a cold Sunday waiting for our Patriots to play. I was so good at making tailgate food for our girl's college field hockey and lacrosse teams. Every Friday night during their seasons, for a five-year stretch, I'd make a huge tin of chicken Caesar bow tie pasta salad and never have any leftovers. Usually I had to make two batches since our girls went to different colleges. Funny; during that time my husband and I had to split up and each attend one of their games. They played against one another in the same conference. I knew we were good parents when our two girls hugged and kissed each other at the game. All throughout playing their sports they both celebrated each other's athleticism and relished their successes. I really miss those days. It's been five years.

One of the happiest things I've done in my life was coach eight years of JV field hockey and lacrosse at a local high school. I loved the players and I think they really liked me too. They still keep in touch. My best players graduated this year and I'm proud to report several are playing their sport in college.

I have to laugh because I am always inventing household projects. My husband will compliment my ideas but always says, "So how much will this cost?" If only he could understand how much money we saved by my purchasing a power saw and repairing our patio pillars. Or by installing our own pavers in our entrance way. Or by painting every inch of our home interior. Or by slipcovering two couches and one chair with painter's drop cloths from Home Depot. I just can't stop thinking there isn't anything I can't do. I love having projects in my life, especially when my results are so satisfying to me and others.

The pink bow on each of my packages is a constant daily part of my life. I've tied it in a knot to keep my family and friend relationships strong. Two of my best friends are my daughters. I'm proudest of my transition from having such influence on the girls' life choices to now enjoying all that they are making happen for themselves. All three of us respect one another. We realize our visits are short and few but very special each time we gather. We talk or text with each other 24/7. I am grateful that they both like me and welcome me into their lives as their friend. For this I am proud to be their mom and a best friend.

I don't think I would be where I am today without all my girlfriends. They are my check and balance. They bring me such happiness and good crying laughs. I remember the time when one of my friends said you have to work hard to have friends and keep them. You have to take the lead sometimes and reach out and plan the gatherings. You need to remember to always know that maybe they are going through things that aren't perfect and offer kindness, love and support. Mostly, I remember that just because I don't hear from a friend for a long time doesn't mean we still aren't friends. They are just as busy as me and whenever we are able to be together we will have a fabulous time catching up.

Overall, I am blessed to have a package filled with incredible presents and sealed with a very tight beautiful pink bow. I realize I am unable to see what's ahead for me in my senior years but I am trying to savor the moment. I yearn for experiences now rather than things to wear or look at. My valuables are my packages. I welcome each and every one of them. When my day as a unique senior is done and I close the lid and tie the bow I will look back and feel so proud of all the incredible things I have accomplished and all the people whose lives I have touched.

When my sister asked me if I would like to work with her on this project I was flattered. I was also thrilled because I really needed something to help me understand the changes I was experiencing. I am excited to be reaching out to women and learning of their challenges and successes as they navigate their seasoned years. This takes a lot of listening and I believe I am good at that. I was the quiet one sitting around the dining table growing up but little did everyone know I was taking it all in. I learned fast what to do and what not to do while my parents attempted to raise all five girls.

Just as I remember Marilou always being the smart one growing up. She had her path all planned and without blinking an eye stepped up to the podium to receive degree after degree and present speech after speech. In addition to being one of the most accomplished woman I know she is also extremely kind and hilariously funny. This is the type of woman I enjoy being around. So now I am privileged to be able to share time with my sister. She makes me laugh so much. She turns any slight negative situation into a humorous one. Her kindness is like a faucet that you can't turn off.

My fondest memories were of the times she guided me into my pre-adolescent years. She was my guardian angel when I needed one most. I only have one sad memory of Marilou and that was when I was visiting her with our two daughters who were 5 and 3 at the time. So approximately 24 years ago. I vividly remember her making us her famous bagel French toast. Then I saw it. She was getting old! She had to put on glasses to cook. I was in disbelief. I needed her to stay young so she could always be there for me. And then I realized I, too, was going to have to wear the same pair of peepers someday. Yes, I am right behind her but closer than ever. Now we are both grown women over 60 searching to find comforting scenarios and solutions for all our sisters. I hope to give her my best effort in this project and help her achieve another strong voice that will resonate amongst all our sisters in this world.

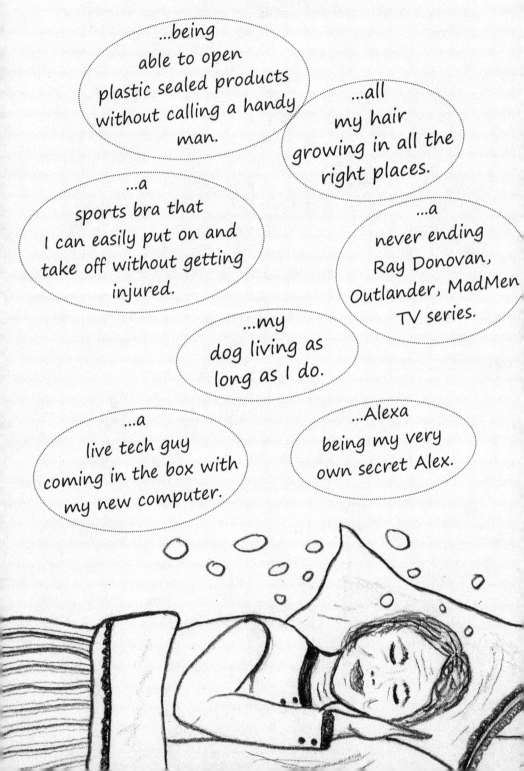

WHY YOU SHOULD READ THIS BOOK

EXTRA, EXTRA, READ ALL ABOUT IT!

70-Year-Old Woman Runs 7 Marathons on 7 Continents in 7 Days

Seventy-year-old Chau Smith wanted to challenge herself even further, so she decided to run seven marathons in seven days on seven continents. In January, the Missouri woman accomplished that goal. Between January 25 and January 31, 2017 Smith ran marathons in Perth, Australia; Singapore; Cairo; Amsterdam; Garden City, New York; Punta Arenas, Chile; and King George Island, Antarctica. Each day, Smith woke up and ran 26.2 miles. Then she'd get on a plane and fly to the next destination to do it all over again.

Source: https://www.cnn.com/2017/03/15/health/70-year-old-marathon-seven-continents/index.html

73-Year-Old Becomes Oldest Woman to Climb Mount Everest

A 73-year-old Japanese woman became the oldest woman to climb Mount Everest breaking her own 10-year-old record. Tamae Watanabe reached the top of the 8,848-meter (29,028 feet) peak at 7 a.m. Watanabe climbed Everest from the northern slope in Tibet-China and started on her final part of her climb at 8:30 p.m. Friday leaving the 8,300-meter staging area with three Sherpas. The final push to the summit was made at night because it becomes very windy after mid-morning.

Source: https://www.cnn.com/2012/05/19/world/asia/nepal-everest-cimb/index.html

68-Year Old Woman Swam from Cuba to Florida in 53 Hours

In 2013 at the age of 64, Diana Nyad became the first person to swim 110 miles from Cuba to Florida without the aid of a shark cage. It took her about 53 hours. After years of training, four failed attempts, being stung by multiple box jellyfish, dealing with dehydration, hypothermia, naysayers and more, she did it.

Source: https://www.theinertia.com/good/this-68-year-old-woman-once-swam-from-cuba-to-florida-in-53-hours/

94-Year-Old is Oldest Woman to Finish Half-Marathon

Harriett Thompson, 94, became the oldest woman to finish a half-marathon Sunday, according to organizers of the San Diego Rock 'n' Roll Marathon. A two-time cancer survivor, Thompson finished in 3 hours, 42 minutes, 56 seconds. She also set a world record in 2015 at the San Diego Rock 'n' Roll Marathon, becoming the oldest woman to complete a full marathon.

https://www.usatoday.com/story/sports/olympics/2017/06/04/94-year-old-oldest-woman-finish-half-marathon/102492406/

99-Year-Old Woman Graduates from College

At 99 years old, Daniels has lived through a number

of watershed moments in American History including the Great Depression, World War II, the Civil Rights movement, the moon landing and the rise of the Digital Age. All of these events pale in comparison to what she describes as the most gratifying moment of her life. Daniels graduated from College of the Canyons in Santa Clarita, California, earning an associate degree in social sciences.

https://www.usatoday.com/story/news/nation-now/2015/06/08/99-year-old-woman-graduates-from-college/28701339/

BALANCING ACT

Too many of my friends have fallen and broken their leg or sprained their ankle. My best friend just recovered from major back surgery and was well on her way to recovery when she took a dive in a dark parking garage and ended up wearing a boot for half a year. I heard about this tip recently so every day I stand on one foot for at least a minute; then balance on the other foot for the same amount of time. At first I was only able to stand on one foot for less than 20 seconds. But after a few months of doing this activity I was able to stand on one foot for at least two minutes. I read in AARP that working on one's balance could potentially minimize falling. Really, practice this one, even if you are out walking your dog. You can stand on one foot waiting for your pup to end one of his sniff parties.

Carla (62)

A few more to get you inspired...

Laura Ingalls Wilder, author of the "Little House on the Prairie" book series, was 64 when she published her first work, *Little House in the Big Woods*, in 1932. She went on to write the next seven books in the Little House series, which became American children's classics and a popular TV series.

❧

Susan B. Anthony was past the age of 80 when she formed the International Woman Suffrage Alliance.

❧

In 1979, Mother Theresa received the Nobel Peace Prize at age 69 for her work with "Missionaries of Charity," a world-wide organization that helped the sick, the poor, the dying, and disaster victims through a network of religious houses, schools, hospices, and charity centers in more than 120 countries.

❧

Anna Mary Robertson Moses, better known as "Grandma Moses", did not start painting until she was 76 years old, after her arthritis made it too hard for her to hold an embroidery needle. Even though she had no formal training, she painted every day for 25 years and produced thousands of paintings. Her simple depictions of farm life were shown all around the world. She died at age 101.

❧

At age 95, Nola Ochs became the oldest college graduate when she received a bachelor's degree from

Fort Hays State University, Kansas in 2007. She didn't stop there – she went on to pursue a Master's degree as well.

❧

At age 75, cancer survivor Barbara Hillary became one of the oldest people, and the first black woman, to reach the North Pole.

❧

Keiko Fukuda was still teaching judo and self-defense classes at age 98, despite having bad knees and Parkinson's disease. In 2011, she became the first woman to ever attain a 10th-degree black belt, judo's highest honor.

❧

92-year-old track-and-field champion Olga Kotelko holds more than 20 world records for track-and-field events, and doctors continue to study her extensively because of her enduring physical prowess.

❧

Lifelong yoga enthusiast Tao Porchon-Lynch fell and broke her hip at age 87, requiring a hip replacement surgery. Her doctor told her she would have to slow down and take it easy on herself – advice that she did not take to heart. A month after her surgery, she began taking ballroom dancing lessons and at age 93 was winning dancing competitions and still teaching 12 yoga classes a week.

❧

SHOW ME THE STATS!

The accomplishments and determination shared above clearly demonstrate as women, we can do anything, at any age. The possibilities are unlimited. For many it is easy and dangerous to create stereotypes about people over the age of 65 and these women heroes clearly defy those odds. We all know however, that the obstacles and challenges related to health and lifestyle as we grow older can be all encompassing. The data shared below are not stereotypes; they are facts-no fake news; just the facts.

POPULATION

There were 47.8 million people ages 65 and older in the United States on July 1, 2015. This group accounted for 14.9 percent of the total population. The age 65 and older population grew 1.6 million from 2014. In 1900 there were just 3.1 million.

Source: Vintage 2015 Population Estimates

INCOME AND POVERTY

The median income of households with householders age 65 and older in 2015 was $38,515.

Source: Income and Poverty in the United States: 2015,

MEDIAN NET WORTH

The median net worth for householders age 65 and older in 2011 was $170,516.

Source: Survey of Income and Program Participation, Net Worth and Asset Ownership of Households: 2011

JOBS

There were 3.7 million women ages 65 and older in the labor force in 2015.

Source: 2015 American Community Survey,

THE GAP

Females significantly outnumber males at older ages, but the gap is narrowing. In 2010, there were 90.5 males for every 100 females among people age 65 and older. "Women outnumber men in the older population at every single year of age," says Werner. In the 2010 Census, there were approximately twice as many women as men beginning at age 89.

http://money.usnews.com/money/retirement/
articles/2012/01/09/65-and-older-population-soars

DISEASE

+ One out of four Americans 65 or older has type 2 diabetes.

Sanja Gupta http://www.everydayhealth.com/sanjay-gupta/type-2-diabetes-and-the-elderly.aspx

+ An estimated 42.2 million American adults over 60 years old have one or more types of Cardiovascular Disease.

http://www.heart.org/idc/groups/heart-public/@wcm/@sop/@smd/documents/downloadable/ucm_319574.pdf

+ "Arthritis is probably the number one condition that people 65 or older contend with," said geriatrician Marie Bernard, MD, deputy director of the National Institute on Aging in Bethesda, Md. It affects about 51 percent of all adults over 65.

http://www.everydayhealth.com/news/
most-common-health-concerns-seniors/

+ 1-in-9 Americans over 65 has Alzheimer's disease

(Alzheimer's Association) http://www.alzheimers.net/resources/
alzheimers-statistics/

+ The likelihood of developing cancer increases with age; approximately 2.15% of all adults over 65 will be newly-diagnosed with cancer each year.

  http://www.seniorhomes.com/p/cancer-facts-for-people-over-50/

+ According to the National Parkinson Foundation (NPF), approximately 60,000 new cases of PD are diagnosed each year. The condition usually affects those over age 65. Approximately 1% of seniors have some form of the disease. http://www.aplaceformom.com/ senior-care-resources/articles/parkinsons-disease-in-the-elderly

+ According to the American Association for the Blind, more than 6.5 million Americans over 65 have a severe visual impairment.

  http://www.aplaceformom.com/
  blog/3-common-causes-of-vision-loss-in-older-people/

SLEEP

A study of adults over 65 found that 13 percent of men and 36 percent of women take more than 30 minutes to fall asleep. Older adults also wake up more often at night than younger adults, primarily to use the bathroom, owing to prostate enlargement in men and incontinence issues in women.

  http://seniorliving.about.com/od/sleep/a/sleep_and_aging.htm

FALLING

One in four Americans aged 65+ falls each year. Every 11 seconds, an older adult is treated in the emergency room for a fall; every 19 minutes, an older adult dies from a fall. Falls are the leading cause of fatal injury and the most common cause of nonfatal trauma-related hospital admissions among older adults.

  https://www.ncoa.org/news/resources-for-reporters/get-the-facts/
  falls-prevention-facts/

A Day in the Life: Deborah, Age 87

7:00	Woke up, make bed, lay on bed a while and talk to Max my pup. Take a short snooze. Get dressed before I go downstairs and make sure I have everything to take downstairs with me for the day.
8:00	Once downstairs, put on a pot of coffee, walk my pup around the complex waiting for coffee to brew.
9:00	Fix pup food, and make my breakfast (same thing every day for years). One green onion, cheese and an egg cooked in the microwave eaten on one slice of bread.
10:00	Read Wall Street Journal, LA Times.
11:00	Take pup for a walk to the park. Water plants and weed small garden in the patio. Instruct my cleaning woman on what needs to be done for the week.
12:00 Noon	Go to the 99 cent store, check the clearance rack, purchase bread and some vegetables.
12:30	Meet my friend for a fine lunch by the sea. Order a glass of chardonnay and some ahi tuna. Friend teaches me how to text on my new iPhone.
2:00	Return home and take a nap on the sofa. Same every day.
4:45	Get pup ready for his walk in the big park. Chat with many of the dog walkers. Hurry back to the car as I can't drive when it gets too dark out.
6:00	Watch the local news, then CNN and Brian Williams my favorite of all. Glad they brought him back.
7:00	Cook dinner while watching the news. Made a small meat loaf for myself. Had a few glasses of wine. Like box wine since it's cheaper than bottled wine and I dilute it with water.

A Day in the Life: Deborah, Age 87

8:00	Have a few more small glasses of wine and call my daughter. Finish up the news and get ready for bed.
9:30	Make sure I have everything I need to take upstairs as I only go up there once a day to sleep. Read my cowboy novel, can't remember the name but it's an excellent read. I have to read light topics or I can't sleep.
10:30	Lights off, Max back on the bed and off to sleep.
11:30	Up to go to the bathroom.
2:00	Wake up, read a bit, fall back to sleep with the light on.
3:30	Back up to go to the bathroom and this continues throughout the night; probably why I am so tired many days.

SLIPPERY SLOPE

As I got older, and I think this is true for most women, our natural lubrication for sexual intercourse decreases. Thank the Lord for my female doctor and her recommendation to begin using a natural lubrication for sex with my husband. Hallelujah is all I gotta say.

Phoenix (63)

OBESITY

Obesity rates among older adults have been increasing, standing at about 40 percent of 65-to-74-year-olds.

https://www.prb.org/aging-unitedstates-fact-sheet/

DEPRESSION

Depression affects more than 35 million adults each year. Of these, 6.5 million are over the age of 65.

http://www.psychguides.com/guides/living-with-depression-in-older-adults/

SUICIDE

The realities of suicide completions in the elderly are staggering. The American Foundation for Suicide Prevention show that there are 14.9 suicides out of every 100,000 people over 65 in the United States. This may seem like a small amount of difference, but with the number of seniors in the United States growing as a result of aging baby boomers, this rate is significant. According to the U.S. Census Bureau, there are 75.4 million baby boomers. If elderly suicide rates remain the same that means that more than 11,000 lives will be lost to suicide annually.

http://seniorsmatter.com/suicide-rates-in-the-elderly/by boomers reach 65 and older.

ISOLATION

According to the U.S. Census Bureau 11 million, or 28% of people aged 65 and older, lived alone at the time of the census. More than one-fourth of women ages 65-74 lived alone in 2014 and this share jumps to 42% among women ages 75-84 and to 56 percent among women ages 85 and older.

https://www.aplaceformom.com/blog/10-17-14-facts-about-senior-isolation/

SUBSTANCE ABUSE

More than 1 million individuals aged 65 or older had a Substance Abuse Disorder in 2014, including 978,000 older adults with an alcohol use disorder and 161,000 with an illicit drug use disorder. Research suggests that substance use is an emerging public health issue among the nation's older adults.

> https://www.samhsa.gov/data/sites/default/files/report_2792/ ShortReport-2792.html

---

ﷺ

NICE WORK IF YOU CAN GET IT

I'm a singer. One thing I've always feared was having a voice that becomes "wobbly" with age or where the vibrato is no longer appealing or beautiful. I began my college career as a music-major and really wanted to learn to play the piano. Well, I've begun vocalizing once a day again and recording myself during every session. I concentrate on pitch and work to even out my vibrato to strengthen my vocal chords, which are like every other muscle in my body. My husband, who plays guitar, and I have begun preparing contemporary Christian songs to perform together. This forces me to concentrate on decreasing the vibrato and blending with his calming, baritone voice. The first time we performed together the audience responded with enthusiastic applause. And, I just enrolled at a local junior college in a piano and theory class. I'm excited to be embarking on my life-time dream of learning to play the piano fluently.

Cheryl (68)

❦

STICKY SITUATION

As I began my career in education, I was headed down a steep learning curve. With so many new experiences I found myself making assumptions all the time. As a teacher, I assumed why my students did not do their work. As a principal, I assumed why some of my teachers did not seem to care as much about their students as I did. As a superintendent, I assumed that everyone I worked with would realize how much I had to offer the profession! When we make assumptions, we believe they are the absolute truth! I have learned that making assumptions causes misunderstandings. Asking honest questions would have been a better way to find out about my students, my teachers, and others in my professional community. Now as I grow older and hopefully wiser, I am focused on making sure I don't make assumptions about people and their motivations too quickly. I don't have time now to be wrong. I ask questions of my doctor, my neighbors, and even my husband since I know it's in me to quickly assume things. I'm still learning though. Just the other day I was in line at Walgreens and this pregnant woman was behind me holding three huge containers of soda. She looked exhausted, so I turned around in line and said, "You can go ahead of me, since you're pregnant." She replied by saying "Thanks… I think I will go ahead but for your information I am not pregnant." I didn't need that embarrassment of feeling so stupid at this stage of life. I know it could happen to the best of us, but really? I need to start taking my own advice.

April (64)

A Day in the Life: Angela, Age 72

6:00	Woke up ecstatic reveling in my husband's golf tournament yesterday, a hard-fought multi-day battle. Celebrated with friends last night and he is contentedly snoozing. Debated whether to get up and make the coffee but opted to stay with the tried and true. He makes the coffee, delivers two cups to me in bed while I in turn eventually make breakfast.
6:15	Awake enough, plug through emails, coffee orders, news and finally look at the addictive game, Words with Friends. Beating my rocket scientist niece is a goal, unfortunately not realized this morning.
6:30	Enjoy having the first cup of coffee in bed while continuing to check on news and weather app for the Cape. We are heading to Rhode Island to visit friends for a couple of nights and want to have an idea of how few or many layers we'll need.
7:00	Complete the daily routine of pill popping (two – one for blood pressure, the other as a post follow-up to breast cancer surgery in 2012). Unfortunately, the doc has not prescribed the anti-aging miracle pill – yet! Work on weights for my arms, a simple workout I try to repeat three times a day, a schedule I've been mostly sticking to for the last month.
7:15	Breakfast of Irish Oatmeal with walnuts and bananas. We start the day in a healthy way – not always finish that way! Check to see how garden looks and if little newly added shubumkins are still alive in the fish pond. So happy to see them.
8:00	Clean! Clean! Clean! Start the 4 loads of laundry while working on cleaning kitchen cabinets, refrigerator, and stove

A Day in the Life: Angela, Age 72

10:00	Another quick arm weight routine and then a shower. Pick up meals from Senior Center and deliver to elderly and shut-ins. Nothing unusual today. We are cautioned to do a wellness check.
12:00 Noon	Stop at Library (yes I still love the library – despite having two Kindles – one borrowed and one recently given as a gift). Notice they have the best 100 books. Decide to pick up A Tree Grows in Brooklyn. Continue on and pick up a few items at the grocery store.
1:00	Lunch of turkey and Swiss cheese on a pita bread for the two of us.
1:30	Work on hooking a rug. Almost finished. Large rug – have been working on it for two years. Not very good at it but a very satisfying project for me.
2:30	Stretch out in office doing crossword puzzles, reading new book and taking a nap.
4:30	Work on newsletter for our business.
6:00	Prep for dinner. Salmon on the grill, corn on the cob, salad and shortbread cookies. Make a gin and grapefruit cocktail. Talk to niece about upcoming high school graduation party and what I should make.
8:00	Watch the remaining two episodes of Billions marveling at how difficult it must be to write, act and produce this show.
10:00	Ah … think of my golf swing … or the golf swing I should be using and drift off … hoping that the magnesium I just took will help with the leg cramps.

❦

STRONGER THAN DIRT

I am almost 90 years old and make it a rule to exercise every single day of my life. Even if I don't feel well I get out my weights and do a few repetitions just to say I exercised for the day. I have a little routine with the weights and then I do some leg lifts and various types of stretching exercises. All told, it's around 20 minutes. I never got involved in yoga but I think this feels like yoga. If there was one thing I would tell women to do in preparation for getting old it would be to work out with some small barbells each day to build up the muscles in your arms. I feel almost as strong as I did twenty years ago. And I can tell that my weight lifting is working because I can still carry 4-5 bags of groceries into the house at once.

Cindy (88)

❦

WHO WORE IT BETTER?

My fashion statement is what I consider current and classy. I guess I don't really dress like most 66 year old women, whatever that means. What draws me to shop say at "Guess" is that it makes me feel like a "Kid in a Candy Store." It makes me feel good because I believe I look good. My leisure time is spent doing what I love versus putting up false barriers that prevent my personal satisfaction. I love rock music. I have attended 40-50 concerts and I don't really think about what the average age of the audience will be. I simply want to go for my own enjoyment. Yes, God Smack, Alice & Chains, Papa Roach are among the few. I love to Rock Out.

Deborah (66)

❧

CALL OF DUTY

AGING is defined in the Standard College Dictionary as "The process of growing mature and old." It is a process we will all go through if we are "fortunate" enough to live that long. Aging is associated in terms of retirement and most of us look forward to the day we retire. When we retire, reality sets in and we quickly learn that retirement is not the great panacea we once thought it was going to be. Many people have trouble with this phase of their life and to solve their frustration they decide to go back to work. I believe there is only one fundamental item every person who is aging must confront as they enter this phase of their life, and that is THE FEELING OF USEFULNESS. During our lifetime we always strived to make something better through work or whatever. Once a person retires we seem to no longer strive to make it better. Not everyone fits this category, but I believe a majority do. My recommendation to everyone retiring is to be aware that after a while you may not feel productive in society. I would recommend you look back over your life and decide what you would like to do to feel useful and engaged in retirement.

I found this out very quickly. I had a wonderful career. When I retired I had a list of items I wanted to accomplish, such as installing automatic sprinklers in the yard and removing plants from my yard and replacing them with something different. Soon I realized these were all short time items and that I better start thinking about what I was going to do for the rest of my life. I think everyone reaches this point at some time after retiring. You look around and see retirees volunteering for every kind of task possible. I personally know people who volunteer at hospitals, substitute teach and work at libraries. Almost everyone I know has made this change, not because of money but to feel important and contribute to something bigger than themselves.

Bobbi (67)

LIVING THE GOOD LIFE!

The average U.S. life expectancy increased from 68 years in 1950 to 79 years in 2013, in large part due to the reduction in mortality at older ages. It's no secret-the stats are daunting and if you were to dwell on them for long you would probably just toss in the towel and give up right here and now. The stats are against us for sure. The good news, however is that the women we interviewed for this book are … yes thriving and not merely surviving. They are thriving despite any unforeseeable barriers or obstacles presented to them. These women clearly told us they want to live a good life, want to embrace life and want to make that life as positive, productive and fun as possible. They also recognized that they belong to one or more of the stat categories presented above. Did it bother them? Clearly. Did it impact their daily lives? Most always. Did it cripple them from enjoying their lives? Absolutely not.

So why should you read this book? This book is not about what can go wrong as you age from decade to decade. The stats are everywhere, we are in the race for our lives. Rather this book posits that each decade, each month, each day, with a little work and deliberate focus can be a positive and engaging experience. The caveat… it takes some work and due diligence. The women interviewed were very generous. They all shared their personal stories, secrets, approaches and strategies for self-fulfillment and happiness while navigating the second half of life. As one of the authors of this book and interviewers I learned so much from these women; I can barely keep up with what they had to offer. For example, I now climb stairs instead of taking the elevator. I used to avoid them like the plague; too high, too many steps which would take all my energy. Or so I thought until I started climbing stairs instead of taking the elevator. Don't get me wrong, there were days when my right knee had a mind of its own, so of course I would take the easy way up. But after a few months of taking the stairs, I felt myself getting stronger each week.

My personal 'ah ha' moment-was that of falling. So many of the women interviewed shared their stories about falling, or as they prefer to call it, *tripping over something.* All agreed, falling can be the death Nell to happiness. Falls result in broken legs, hospital stays and can take away the joy of living. Again, it's well known throughout the research that as one ages we don't lift our feet as high above the ground when walking as when we were younger. Just a few minutes ago I saw my neighbor, Betty, leaving her house sporting a wrist cast. I believe she's around 70 or so. *What happened,* I asked? Her story, was a sad one that included two grueling surgeries, pins and metal plates. She showed me three visible aluminum pins sticking up from all sides of her cast. She told me she wished she hadn't looked up at the men cutting palm trees when crossing the

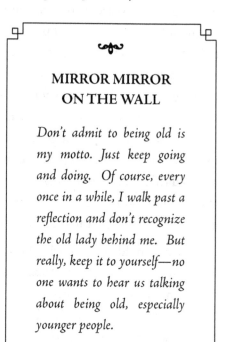

MIRROR MIRROR ON THE WALL

Don't admit to being old is my motto. Just keep going and doing. Of course, every once in a while, I walk past a reflection and don't recognize the old lady behind me. But really, keep it to yourself—no one wants to hear us talking about being old, especially younger people.

Judy (77)

street to the Del Coronado Hotel. Not paying much attention to her immediate surroundings, her sneaker caught a fixture in the road and caused her to fall hard onto the pavement, crushing her right arm with the bulk of her body. She broke three bones in a variety of places. "This has been pure hell. I can't even open up a container of yogurt without help. I'll have this damn thing on for another six weeks," she moaned.

Now, because of her story this morning as well as the cautionary "tripping" advice from our interviewees, I walk with a purpose, try not to rush, be present and above all practice my balance every day.

My sister was also changed by this book after interviewing countless women on the East Coast. She recently shared that one woman turned the table on her during the interview and asked what she was afraid of when approaching old age. She responded by saying that she was fearful she would not be able to see her daughters get married (since they are both single and travelling the world and trying out many different things in their lives). My sister worried her children would not have children in time for her to participate in their future enjoyments, successes and special moments. Her interviewee cautioned that things are very different now; women have all sorts of choices regarding how they live their lives that women did not have "back in the day". This woman also advised my sister that she may not have what she personally has enjoyed in her life. "It just doesn't happen like that anymore," she warned. "Your children have so many choices now and so much time to make them. You will not see 7-10 grandchildren like I have experienced. But with these 7-10 more people in your family comes the worries and tribulations of so many young people navigating their lives. Things you see and hear about them may not always be pleasant. Everything comes with a price". My sister later explained that she was overcome with emotion and had an incredible feeling of relief. This was the way it was going to be. Perhaps she was approaching a 'new normal' and she could live with this. Her family was perfect and beautiful just the way they were. "We are coasting, she said. "The four of us share every day with one another. So I'm now content to sit back and enjoy what is to come. I know I will be blessed and fortunate for the moment. I now understand and guess I am learning a lot about myself and how to navigate the rest of my life".

So why should you read this book? Hopefully you will find some stories that resonate with you. Perhaps you too will read a secret or two and find something that will change the way you view your world. Most importantly, we hope that some of these secrets, interviews and cartoons will put a smile on your face and perhaps bring you to a new way of thinking. I loved reading the Day in a Life scenarios. Why? Because they showed me that not every 60-80 year old woman is home writing the great American novel, swimming the English Channel or hosting a local cooking television show. They helped me to understand that we are ordinary women, women doing the basic routines of life, and having some fun. It showed me my life is comparable to these women, a comforting thought after a short spin through Facebook, Instagram and other social media can often make me feel like I am the only one not celebrating life. Thank you to all these women who took time to meet with us and share their lives, hopes and dreams with other women in the world. I am confident through their generous donation of time and spirit their stories and advice will resonate and make a small difference for other women navigating their own challenges and journeys throughout the aging process.

UNDER THE MATTRESS

I always worry about everything now that I am getting older. I especially worry about the power grid going down and having no cash on hand to purchase food or medicine should stores not be able to process our debit cards. Advice to women [and men] stash some cash somewhere in your house just in case. Just in case of an earthquake, a flood, or fire. After all I live in California and we have had three major disasters in my lifetime. I want to be able to stand in line with some hard-core cash for my wine and Xanax should we go off the grid for an extended period of time.

Martha (67)

❧

THE ULTIMATE DRIVING MACHINE

I was an avid bike rider when I was younger and then continued riding some type of bike throughout my adult life for exercise and fun. Then one day, without any warning both knees gave out and trust me, that was a very sad day. I believed life as I knew it was over. I was feeling really sorry for myself about my lack of mobility and then one day saw this older man riding a bike down the street at an unusual fast speed for his age. I later learned he was riding an electric bike. Ah ha... I thought, my answer to bad knees. It didn't take me long to check out one for myself and purchased a baby-blue beach cruiser that soars through the air like a bird. Every once in a while when I'm riding, I get the stare from younger people but lately I see more and more people my age riding these bikes. If you love riding a bicycle, I would highly recommend purchasing one if you can afford it. Riding my electric bike has given me a whole new outlook on life. And yes, don't forget to wear a helmet!

Cheryl (63)

❧

OH MY ACHING BACK

Everyone aches, everyone has pain. Every time you tell someone you are hurting or they tell you the same, then it brings all that pain to the front of your mind and you hurt more. Think about when you're reading, watching a movie or thinking about something you like doing; you forget your aches for a while. That is one of the biggest reasons not to bring it up.

Judy (77)

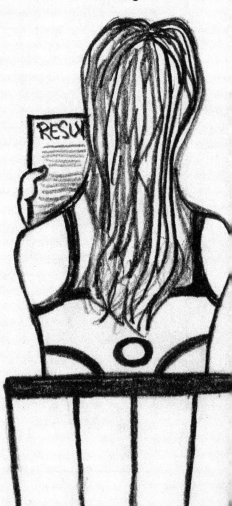

UP CLOSE
and PERSONAL

Liz, Age 67

As I walk to Liz's home I am wondering what she might prepare for lunch. When I approached her about being interviewed for our project, she said she'd love to prepare something to eat for us. She told me she would be finishing her yoga class and would need to eat something because she scheduled another activity after our meeting. Liz greets me at her front door with a huge smile and embrace. The entrance is elegantly blooming with Hydrangeas and colorful perennials. Liz is very proud of her one-year old garden which I compliment for its maturity.

Liz, 67 years old, is a petite woman with exquisitely coiffed, short red hair. She reminds me of those cute pixies in school everyone loved and doted on. Liz shared she has always been lucky to eat anything she wants and never have to watch her weight. The table has been set in advance for our visit. Together, we enjoy chicken salad and crackers. Delightful. I admire all the Irish memorabilia throughout her home and think to myself, there's definitely some heritage going on here. I'm also attracted to a Penn State football item and learn of Liz's and her husband's fond loyalty to the Penn State Lions. She informs me they frequent Penn's football games religiously. I visually graze the inside of her home and am slightly envious of Liz's neat, orderly, and tidy surroundings, much like her own appearance. I make a mental note to remember to streamline and purge my own knickknacks when I return home. After lunch Liz clears the table. This is my cue to begin an informal conversation with Liz. I look forward to sharing her private means to a healthy, happy and wise life. I savor this moment and am thankful for her time and willingness to participate.

Could you share something you did when you were younger that contributed to your good health today?

I always exercised throughout my life and for about the past 10 years I've been taking yoga. I think has helped me dramatically. I try to walk every day. I've done that throughout my entire adult life. I'm always exercising. I use weight bearing machines, I do stretches, floor exercises, that sort of thing. I go to a gym on a regular basis.

Is there something you did in your younger years you are paying for now?

Oh yes, sunbathing out in the sun. Being very fair skinned, I always tried to get a tan. I didn't use sunscreen. I am paying for that right now. I've had a few skin cancers and a lot of precancerous conditions on my face, so, now I must have medical facials. So, yes, that was something I really regret. I'm Irish on both sides of my family and very fair skinned.

Can you describe any activities you are currently doing that influence your health today? You mentioned Yoga and walking.

I meditate. I have high blood pressure, but it's controlled. I found a machine called RESPeRATE; it's a program involved with toned musical terms that help you with your breathing. What happens is you do 15 minutes every night and your breathing rate is lowered throughout those 15 minutes. I asked my doctor and she said, "Whatever you're doing, it's working," because now my blood pressure is lower. I am still on medication because that was part of my background. Genetically, my mother and my grandmother both had high blood pressure and it wasn't anything to do with their weight. It is because we were all small women. It's just hypertension. I find this RESPeRATE really helps.

Do you practice this in your home?

Yes, I do it here in my home. It's a little tiny machine. You put a belt around your abdomen that monitors your respiration rate and then the tone is set. You then try to lower your breathing.

I'm glad to hear it's helping you. Do you have any advice for women to maintain their good health?

Practice yoga. I had arthritis in my knee because of an injury when I was much younger. With the Yoga, I have been able to stay away from getting knee replacements. I think the flexibility has helped a great deal.

Can you share any downsides of getting older and how you're dealing with them?

Well, I try to maintain a very healthy weight. I think probably that's the only thing I am a little upset about. I find as you get older, you put on a few pounds. It's harder and harder to get rid of those few pounds. Do I diet? No. I still like to have my afternoon tea and cookie, so I haven't taken that away from myself. That's the only thing I worry about. I know a lot of people try to get cosmetic surgery and things like that. I wouldn't ever go near that. I'm going to try to age gracefully. I'm not averse to make up, but I would never do anything to try to alter my appearance.

Any special advice about aging you would like to give women?

Be satisfied. Just be satisfied. When you look in the mirror, smile. I think a smile goes a long way to help you be satisfied with your looks. Don't worry about the wrinkles or getting old.

What is your special trick to look so good?

I don't know that I do!! I drink a lot of water. I take a daily vitamin every day. I basically keep active and get facials, medical facials.

What about alcohol?

I drink wine. I like red wine. I think it makes me healthy.

Can you describe a recent time in your life that made you feel beautiful and young again?

Well let me think. My husband compliments me a lot. My niece, when I told her I was 67, she said, "No, you're only 50". I said, *Oh, I love you.*

What spiritual areas, if you don't mind sharing, guide you through this phase of your life?

I've always been a Catholic, a Roman Catholic. I have always gone to church once a week. It's necessary for me to go and have that quiet hour in church. I'm spiritual. I pray a lot. I try to say the rosary every night before I go to bed. I feel an afterlife. I feel that I'm living a good life, and that things will be good.

When you hear the word wealth, what does that mean to you?

Again, I think of the word 'satisfied' ... that you're satisfied with what you have. That you don't want for anything.

How are you keeping up with the changing world of finance as a woman?

I hate to admit this, but my husband handles this. He was in the financial industry and has taken care of everything. He's done a marvelous job. The only thing I do is keep a budget. I try not to go overboard, but my husband has really taken on all the financial parts of our lives. I know that we have long term health insurance, everything. He has taken care of everything. I hate to say that I have not tried to look into that too much. He follows the stock market every day. I just know if it is up or down.

A lot of women have told me that they have a secret stash of cash? Do you have anything that you stashed away for yourself?

No, I use a credit card.

Do you have any advice for women entering their sixties on how to be prepared financially?

I think, and I was raised this way too, I shouldn't say that it's just because of my husband, but I was raised that you should always have some security. You should always have some money set aside so you will be able to withstand any problems. So, yes, I have delayed gratification. If we want something big, we don't rush into it immediately; we think about it. We save towards it and then eventually can do what we want.

What kind of things do you do for yourself to keep your mind working?

I'll tell you, I probably have risks because my mother had dementia and my father had Parkinson's. So, neurologically, I have two strikes against me. I try to keep active with my mind every day. I do the cross-word puzzles in the newspaper. I read the newspaper every morning. It usually takes me about an hour and a half. I am in a book club. I find that quite stimulating because it's not always books I would pick up to read. I like to read different types of books but always read the book assigned. There hasn't been one book since 2004 that I did not finish from start to end. I will always finish the book, even if I don't like it. I feel like I can get something out of every book. I was a teacher. Sometimes I think I am too positive. My outlook is always to be positive. I've been told this by my husband that I always look for the good in everything. That's the way I like to live. That's what I believe is a healthy way to live. I love to play bridge. All of those things combined keep my brain working.

Some women have had difficult experiences but have learned important lessons from them. Is this true for you?

Yes, I think one thing that was difficult was taking care of my parents when they were ill. What did I learn? I learned that time is so precious. Even when it gets the darkest, and you think this is never going to end, it does end. When it does, know that you've done your best. Have no regrets. I can honestly say that I have no regrets.

Can you tell me what you think the secret is to a happy marriage?

I think my husband and I are very well-suited personality wise. We very rarely fight. When we disagree we eventually talk it out and things are okay. There is no time when we won't talk to one another, or slam the door, or give each other the silent treatment. We don't let things get to us.

What would you say about living a happy and successful life that you didn't know when you were 20 or 30 years old?

I didn't know that time would go so quickly. Now that I look back on it, I mean I still feel like I'm in my thirties. I know that's not true. In fact, I just said to my husband today, *there are a lot of people in our community that are becoming sick.* Then I thought, *Gee, you know, there's been a death recently.* That hit me hard saying it up front. Now that I see it happening I say, *Hey, I'm not far behind.* So, I don't know. I think there are a couple more goals I want to accomplish. I better get going.

As you look back over your life, do you see any turning points as a key event or experience that changed the course of your life or set you on a different track?

Wow. This goes way back. I never wanted to be a teacher and I became one mainly because of the time I was living in. You were either a teacher or a nurse. Don't get me wrong, I had the most rewarding career. When I look back on it, and the things that I accomplished, I'm very proud of what I did. When I see young girls today in business, running businesses, and having all these incredible careers, I think to myself, *Gee, I would liked to have tried that.* There weren't many women in business when I started my career.

Yes, a lot of women comment they felt they were limited when choosing a career.

Yes, for sure. However, when I look back, I think of all those children I came across as a teacher. Eventually, you see families or the kids themselves and they tell you what a difference you made in their life.

What do you do for fun now that you're retired? What makes you happy?

I travel quite a bit. I'll tell you, after taking trips, I always say, *There's no place like home.* I'm always happy to return home. We have a beautiful house with lovely surroundings. My husband and I both have similar interests. That's another reason why our marriage is successful. I think I took up golf because he was such an avid golfer. I remember when we were getting married, my mother said to me, "I think you better take up that hobby." She was right, because a lot of our vacations revolve around golf. We both enjoy it. We have a lot of similar interests.

Sounds like golf is the glue to your marriage. What do you fear most about getting old and how do you address that fear?

I think I've already mentioned how it bothers me that people around me are getting ill, that concerns me. I don't have much I can do about that. That's part of growing older. I try to stay as healthy as possible.

What would you say are the major values or principles you live by?

To be kind and to treat others the way I want to be treated, you know, the Golden Rule. Oh, and one more thing I am working on right now. I'm trying not to gossip. I'm trying to stay out of gossip. I've told my friends if someone says something about me, please don't repeat it. I like to live in my own bubble. People are good. They are most of the time. When they are very nice to my face that works for me. I don't want to know the gossip. I'm going to keep inside that little bubble.

What advice would you give a woman that's just entering her sixties?

Live each day to the fullest. Yes, that's it. Live each day to its fullest. I have really enjoyed this time together talking about aging. Thank you for asking me these questions.

⚜

SKIP THE PITY PARTY

I live alone and sometimes it can get plain lonely in this house. Yes, my kids call me every day but there was a point in my life a few years ago when I was getting really depressed on a regular basis… kind of like one might feel on a rainy day that continued for weeks. Then one day I read an article in the paper that said loneliness in older people can cause depression. I'm a fairly smart person and wish I had come to that conclusion on my own and a lot sooner. So what did I do? I started conversations with people on the sidewalks when I would walk my dog. Before I thought they were too busy to talk with me but oddly they also wanted to chat. Then I decided to join a book club in my local town. While I don't think I'll ever become good friends with any of these women since we only meet once a month, just being in a group with others is a huge "high" for me. Then I took the big leap of faith, [my own that is] and joined a gym. I thought I would feel embarrassed at my age to go to the gym with all these young people hanging out but soon learned there's a lot of nice people, and people like me at the gym. I visit about 5 times a week for about 40 minutes and people are getting to know me by name and even say "Hi" when I walk in the door. In retrospect, I should have been doing these activities all along, but guess I just started feeling sorry for myself. I am happy now and make every attempt to get out of the house every day. So, if I see you coming down the sidewalk, you are fair game.

Suzette (65)

A Day in the Life: Nina, Age 70

7:00	Woke up, watched some morning news and checked emails.
7:30	Made an egg white omelet, berry salad and coffee for breakfast.
8:00	Had breakfast with my husband and spoke on the phone with daughter & granddaughters.
9:00	Got showered and dressed.
9:30	Went for a walk with my friend Jo. We walked 2.5 miles and chatted for a little bit afterwards.
10:30	Watered and deadheaded the potted plants on the deck. Did some midweek house cleaning and had lunch.
1:00	Put in my monthly volunteer time at Pregnancy care center.
4:30	Drove back home to meet up with my husband and had a little snack.
5:00	My husband and I headed down to Lexington to watch my 11 year old granddaughter's summer league basketball game. Before the game started, I spent some time with my 8 yr. old granddaughter in the playground.
7:30	On our way back home from the game we stopped at a restaurant for dinner. Had some nice wine and shared a burrada salad and Branzino for dinner.
10:15	Arrived at home and got ready for bed.
10:30	Read and replied to some emails.
11:00	Turned off the lights and went to sleep.

Something about screwing that very large beach umbrella into the sand made 'em all come running to help! Jeanine was so happy she packed enough picnic for two!!

ᥴᠹᥞ

PEACHY QUEEN

After retiring, I had a lot of time on my hands. In keeping with what so many do after retiring, I made a "to do" list. One of those tasks involved cleaning closets and weeding out my wardrobe. As an executive, I always wore a suit to work. Even on 'Casual Fridays I wore black jeans with a sport jacket over a white blouse. Very classy. While taking a cursory inventory of the items in my closet, I noticed a faint smell of body odor in the air. I pulled one suit off the hanger and gave it a major "sniff test." Sure enough my suspicions were true; long days of stress, strain and sweat had found a home in this piece of clothing. I inspected the remaining suits... same thing. In one moment of precise clarity, I began to stuff suit after suit into four large trash bags, loaded them into the car and took them to Goodwill before I could change my mind. My point is that I was finally feeling free from the confines of executive power... that of wearing a suit. Black suits, navy suits, pant suits, $800 suits, suits on sale, suits for slim days, suits for fat days. And two red suits for days when I expected conflict. This personal purging of executive armor while exhilarating, posed a new problem. What do I wear now? I knew I was planning to consult occasionally but also knew I didn't want to be strapped wearing any type of prescribed fashion. I wanted to wear color. I wanted to wear dresses, skirts, artistic jewelry, scarves and hats. I wanted to show my true personality and develop my own fashion sense. It took some time to find a new style but after a few months I began to find my groove by wearing fun, colorful and comfortable clothing. If I could give any advice to women and their appearance as they age is this... wear what you feel good in. Experiment until you find a style that 'suits' you. Wear purple, pink, AND yellow. Be free.

Melanie (67)

◆

GOING ONCE, GOING TWICE

I am attempting to downsize. What exactly does that mean? Well I always thought it meant we would buy a smaller home waking up to palm trees and handing off plenty of our belongings to our children. In a perfect world back in the 70s or maybe 80s it would have worked. I wanted many of the belongings passed on to me by my parents mostly because I couldn't afford to purchase my own bed, couch, dining table and dishes. Today, our daughters have refused most of our belongings. I've tried to pass on wicker chairs, overstuffed chairs, desks, lamps, bedroom sets, framed pictures, linens, dishes and the list goes on. They have their own style and it doesn't include my hand offs. They have a clean, streamlined, simple taste. I celebrate them. I wish I could emulate them now in my 60s. My only way to do that is to purge my environment by selling on eBay, Craigslist or eliminating items on the curb every Tuesday. It makes me sad to give away things that have meaning from the past but I keep reminding myself they are only things. So what is a thing? It is material and does not live on like an experience or moment in my life. It is not an imprint in my mind that I can remember, see or touch. So get rid of it. I will keep the experiences and cherished memories. I will toss the things into the end zone and kick off to my future filled with special events I'll savor forever.

Joan (63)

UP CLOSE and PERSONAL

Sandy, Age 68

Sandy and I were working on a project in Orange County when I told her about our book project on women and aging. She was all over it wanting to be part of it. She agreed to share her thoughts in an interview after returning back to Washington, her current residence. I have known Sandy for years in our roles as school superintendents. I admire Sandy's way of speaking her mind and making sure she stays true to herself and women's issues. Sandy is a gay woman. I learned about that aspect of her life two years ago and must admit I was surprised. Surprised since I didn't know one gay female [or gay male for that matter] who succeeded in navigating the career track to become a school superintendent. I immediately supposed she must be really something to take on that challenge in a field dominated by white males, at least in California. Sandy is a fun person to be around, always positive, outgoing and looking for the bright side of every story in life. She is that 'feel good' type of person you nudge closer to be near when you see her in a room. Thank you, Sandy, for your generous spirit and time donated to this project.

Can you share anything you did when you were younger that has contributed to your good health today?

I was always physically active. When I was younger I was very much into being outdoors. I played a lot of sports and was outside all the time doing something that was physically active. I've always been big on physical exercise. It's a huge, huge, part of my life. I also think the play component fits in here because as a kid you learn a lot of skills that help you to become a functioning adult, things like getting along with people and developing leadership skills.

What sports did you play?

When I was younger the big sport for most of my life, which really carried me through college, was swimming. I was a competitive swimmer from when I was a real small kid until I finished high school. I swam a little bit while in college, but then I didn't have time for it because I had to work. I ended up teaching swimming for years and was able to put myself through college. Then I coached women when I was a high school teacher for a couple of years.

How about something you wish you hadn't done in your younger years that maybe you're paying for now?

I was a runner for a long time. I started running in college and ran until I was running five, six miles a day and sometimes more. I ran a lot of little mini marathons, a few of those 12 milers. On the weekends, it was not uncommon for me to go off and do 10, 12 mile runs, but I blew out some disks in my back. That was a very painful thing I went through when I was 39 years old. I had to have a discectomy, which was a partial removal of the discs and have never been able to run since. So, I wish I hadn't done so much running.

You can't run anymore?

No, I tried a couple of times and it's excruciating afterwards, so, I can't do it. It was about maybe eight or nine years after that I started putting on weight. I was always pretty trim and very muscular. Then, in my 50s, I really started piling the weight on. Then when I became a superintendent I put more weight on. I have taken some of it off but not nearly what it should be. That was a big change for me.

Can you describe any activities you are currently doing that influence your health today?

Walking. We walk every day, three, four miles every day. The only time we don't is when the weather's just so bad, and then I can't do it, which occasionally happens here in Washington, unlike California. We get a lot of rain. Even in the rain, I'm out walking. I've got inclement weather gear. I put on everything, a cap, slicker, slicker pants and waterproof shoes and just go. I believe I'm not balanced if I don't get that physical activity. Walking is a really good way for me to stay active. Walking keeps my back fluid so I don't get back pain. I find if I don't get out and move and exercise rigorously and regularly, I will suffer with back pain 99 percent of the time.

Do you wear a Fitbit or anything like that?

Yes, I have an Apple Watch that records everything. I know exactly how much I'm walking and I've got a chronology of it for the past several years. When I didn't have the Apple Watch, I would carry my phone and use the fitness component in there, so I know how far I walked.

Do you have any special advice for women regarding maintaining good health as they grow older?

You know, making sure you get enough rest and eat well. It's also really important you don't over medicate yourself. I am not on medication much at all. I take just one small dose of a prescription drug for high blood pressure and use a prescribed nasal spray because I have some allergies. I think a lot of people over medicate themselves. That would be my advice. They drink and eat too much and don't exercise. Certainly the company you keep and your frame of mind is important. As I grow older, I have less time for people that don't make me happy. I try to spend my time with people I really appreciate and love and have some commonality with. I also try to spend time with people who are intellectually stimulating as well as kind, considerate and sensitive. I do not want to deal with people that bring me down. I find it makes me a lot happier and a lot more grounded.

Would you describe any barriers you're currently experiencing with your health and how you address those challenges to live a positive life?

I think the one thing that concerns me the most is my weight. I am probably 35, 40 pounds overweight and I don't like that. I try and address it, but I've got to really put my nose to the grindstone to do something to lose weight. I could do it easily, but I have to give up some of the pleasures I like so much. I love to cook and love to try new things. I love to experiment with different things in the kitchen and I love to drink good wine. It's a deadly combination. When you're trying to lose weight no matter how much walking you do and how much you exercise, you really must cut back on calories to make it work. I think that's my biggest detriment. Now that retirement is here, I certainly don't have a problem getting enough sleep. I definitely did when I was working, and it was awful. I was always sleep deprived and I never realized it at the time.

Can you describe how you feel about any changes in your personal appearance and share any thoughts on how you deal with those changes?

I think there's a certain beauty particularly to women as they age. I don't have a problem looking older. Sometimes it kind of fascinates me. I find myself looking in the mirror and I say, *Wow... I look like my grandmother... I look like my mother.* I think it's part evolution of the human being. It's our societal demands that keep people trying to make themselves look more youthful and more beautiful. They run and have face-lifts and have excess surgeries that I think are absolutely ridiculous, unless there's a medical reason for it. I don't have that hang up; it's just not in me. I don't do some of the things I used to do anymore. You know, when I was working I had the clothes, the manicured nails, the highlighted hair and makeup. I don't do any of that anymore and it's perfectly okay with me. It's a much more relaxed state of being and it feels more natural.

We all have a few tricks to keep looking good and to be presentable. Would you mind sharing a few of your tricks if you have any?

One thing I believe in strongly is getting a good haircut. I think sometimes women just let their hair go and it looks horrible. I think investing in someone who really does a good job cutting your hair is super important. Other than that, I think not trying to look like something other than what you are. I'm sure you see this. You see women in our age group dressed like they're still 25. I have this friend, a beautiful woman when she was younger. She was a knockout and now she's 66. She dresses like her 30-year-old daughter and looks completely inappropriate. It is not congruent with who she is. She should just relax and tone it down a bit. She would be a lot classier looking. I think just accepting oneself. Not to say we need to dress like an old woman, but we are old women, and it is what it is.

Can you describe a recent time in your life that made you feel beautiful and young again?

Mary, my spouse's son got married in May. We went to the wedding. We also saw him graduate with his Medical Degree. He graduated from medical school in Washington DC on Saturday and then on Monday, 60 miles away he got married. So we had this incredible whirlwind weekend. It was so refreshing to be around his age group predominantly. It felt really great being around the energy of younger people and having them want to dialogue with me about things going on in their lives. Just being part of a different age group was very uplifting, very rewarding. It made me feel very hopeful about the future, of the certainty of this country, and these young leaders that are going to be taking over the next 10 years. It was a pretty remarkable experience. It wasn't young and beautiful, but more of an emotional thing; being inspired by such a younger group of folks.

We all know wealth comes in all kinds of shapes and sizes. Let's start with the topic of spiritual wealth. What spiritual areas, if you don't mind sharing, guide you through this phase of your life?

Well, I'm kind of agnostic. I'm not really a churchy person. I think the spiritual piece for me is mostly nature, the beauty I find where I live. There's an abundance of it. There's hardly a day that goes by I don't see something that just knocks me out. It's just an amazing place to be. We see eagles out the front window here constantly. I think that's really my spiritual sense. It's more what I get from the calm and serenity of nature. Music centers me the same way too as does exercise.

When you hear the word wealth, what does that mean to you and how would you define wealth at this stage of your life?

It is definitely not money. To me, wealth is the abundances you have in your life that make you happy. You know, it's your health, it's a peace. It's a sense of calm, it's being loved and having the ability to love someone else. It's a strong network of family and friends. To me that's wealth. That's abundance.

Can you describe any strategies you currently use to keep up with the changing world of finance?

I have a really good financial advisor and I trust this guy implicitly.

So you don't worry about finances, you just rely on him?

Pretty much. I mean, we discuss it certainly and he will entertain my ideas about how much risk we want to take, all those kinds of things. For the most part, I trust his judgment. I've been doing this for a long time and he's really good.

We've been reading about women who disclose they keep a secret stash of cash on hand just for themselves, for any reason. Have you ever?

I don't. I have never. The relationship I have is a very transparent one and those areas about finances are shared.

What is the main thing you do to save money during this phase of your life?

Oh, right now, that's not happening because everything's going to the new house we're building. We do look for things on sale and we are sharp consumers. If it's something we want to get, we get it. Fortunately, we have the resources to do that. I think being wise consumers, especially on big things and not being cheap by any means. Being thoughtful about your major expenditures, like how you buy a car and when you really need it, that kind of stuff is important.

Do you have any advice for women about saving money or spending money?

One thing I look back on was that I put a good chunk of my money into retirement accounts when I was working. I started making substantial money later in my career, so I sheltered a lot of that money. Honestly, I wish I had tightened my belt a little bit more and put more in. I think I should have done that. I certainly made some really good decisions financially and I'm not hurting. I could've had that cushion be a little bit more right now if I had been a little wiser about saving. Part of the reason is I always struggled with money. I grew up in a poor family and put myself through college. I was the first one in my family to go to college and I always had to work. Any money I made during that time I burned. So, for me, when I finally got a little bit of extra money, I didn't have to worry about it anymore. I indulged in things that probably in retrospect I should have thought a little bit more about.

Can you share anything out of the ordinary that you do to keep your mind working?

Oh yes, I'm taking piano lessons. I'm also a pretty decent guitarist. I've been playing guitar since I was 10 years old. I read chords and tablature, I don't read notes. I've always wanted to learn to play piano and I've always wanted to be able to sight read music. I have a high musicality but I didn't play piano. We have this incredibly beautiful grand piano. Talk about exercising your brain! It's pretty remarkable. You know, you've got to be able to read two sets of staff and coordinate everything, use two hands and make it all match. I can just feel the synapses wiring. It's really an amazing thing. I'm also an avid reader and it's not uncommon for me to blow through a book in a week. I'm reading the Bob Woodward book right now.

Some people mention they have had a difficult or stressful experience, but have learned important lessons from them. Is there any stressful experience you can share that you've learned from?

Well, my first partner and I were together for 20 years. We got together when I was 26 years old and when I was 46 she took off with a friend of ours. I was totally devastated for a year, maybe more. It was the most gut-wrenching thing I'd ever been through. In the long run, I look at that period of time as the biggest growth, personally, that I think I've ever had. I had to completely redo my life and reformat everything. I had to figure out how I was going to operate in a world without her. It took a long time for me to get over the pain and the anger. I've since let it all go. We're good friends now and it's fine. It was a learning experience for me to regroup as a single person. For gay people that are operating in a professional realm, especially during that time when everybody was really in the closet, it was scary for me. I thought, oh my God, I'm going to be by myself for the rest of my life. I can't imagine this. Where am I going to find somebody? I don't even know how to go about it. You look around at some of the women I knew who were out and I thought, *Oh Yuk are you kidding me? Never in life.* Eventually, I met a whole new set of friends and marched on and grew a lot from it. I went to a therapist and learned a lot about myself and probably that was the most difficult thing I've ever had to deal with.

That leads me to the next question. Can you share the secret to a happy marriage or relationship?

We talk about everything. There's no conflict with us that's not addressed openly and resolved in some form or another, whether it be a compromise or one person saying, "Oh, I'm wrong, let's do it your way." It's discussed, and we spend a lot of time talking about stuff like that. It's important especially when you're going through something that's a combined experience like building a house. This is where you're combining resources you both spent a lifetime building up into a joint venture. It can create a lot of stress and so far we've done really well. I just think open communication and being transparent and not stuffing your emotions, thinking they're going to go away because they never do. They just explode later on.

What would you say you know now about living a happy and successful life you didn't know when you were 20 or 30?

That's really a tough one. I think for me probably it's don't sweat the small stuff so much. I used to get bothered by things I thought at the time were huge and now they're just so insignificant. I think part of that has come from the realization that we have a finite period of life on this planet. In the last three years I have been the executor for two of my friends who have passed away that were very close friends. I was the person that had to go through all their belongings, sell their houses and divide things up. Settling their estates and working with the attorneys really opened my eyes to making sure that every day is what I believe it is, a gift. I think when you're younger you don't realize that.

You talked a lot about playing piano and walking. What else makes you happy?

We spend a lot of time at the beach. I *love* the beach here. We can go down to the beach below where we're building. We own all the way down to the water. Can you believe that you can own a beach in Washington? You can't own a beach in California, but in Washington, you can. I think that's awful someone can own a beach, but nevertheless, there's never anybody there. We can walk for miles on the beach and rarely run into another person. So, that's my sense of spirituality and that's something that makes me really happy. We love doing that. I also spend a lot of time with my dogs. I love my dogs. I go everywhere with them. They are my constant companions.

What do you fear most about getting old and how do you address that fear?

I think losing independence. That's as scary as it gets. My mother's still alive and she's 92. I'm an only child and she lives in assisted living in Port Townsend. So, I go see her and in order to do that I have to get on the ferry once a week and that's a whole day. She can hardly walk anymore because she has issues with her back. It's affected her mobility and legs. She walks with a walker and when I take her outside, it's in a wheelchair... that's kind of scary. She's lost her ability to go out and go shopping and do the things she was so vibrant about. This happened about seven or eight years ago. Losing mobility is a scary one. To address that fear I make sure I walk and work on keeping my balance and making sure I'm fit. Certainly, being overweight doesn't help. That's kind of why I'm freaked out a little bit today because I can't really see after having cataract surgery yesterday. Today I wonder what it would it be like if my eyesight was like this all the time. This would be horrible. Losing control is not a pleasant sight.

What would you say are the major values or principles you live by today?

Honesty is number one, right up there. I can't tolerate people that are full of bull. I just can't do it. I think being generous with your time and resources is big to me. Giving back. You know, we have people that mentored and supported us. It is really cool to be in that position. To be able to be the one giving back. Hopefully we are passing on some of our life lessons to them that will help them avoid some of the pitfalls we experienced.

Now that you know what 60 looks like and feels like what advice would you give younger woman approaching their senior years?

I think women need to be more forceful in asking for what they're worth and demanding more equality. I think the time is so right. I was looking at the news a little while ago about this whole thing with Kavanaugh. Last night I saw the replay of that whole thing with Anita Hill and it just blew me away. Then I thought, how on earth have I forgotten the big pieces of time with Anita Hill and then I put it in today's context. There's no way in hell that Clarence Thomas should be on the Supreme Court. No way. We were complacent, and I think women have a much bigger voice than what they are allowing themselves to feel. The Women's March in January of 2017 that occurred on the day of the inauguration was big. I participated in the march in Seattle. I have never had an experience like that in my whole life. I went through a lot of anti-Vietnam stuff and other demonstrations when we were in college, but nothing like this. I think we're almost at a tipping point where if women would continue to band together and be more forceful and actually demand equality, we would begin to see some of these things shift. That would be my advice. Don't, just don't sit back and wait for it to happen. Get out there and take over. Make it equitable, make it fair. Level that playing field.

COMFORT DOG POLICY UPGRADE

Lucille was so excited to learn about FLY AWAY AIR'S Husband Comfort Plan. She immediately booked Jack's seat for $50.00 and left Sparky home with a sitter.

◦⊙◦

LOOK MA, NO FOOD OR WATER

I know this sounds like I'm being an alarmist and not what you're looking for in this book, but I think it makes sense to think ahead and get prepared in case of an emergency. One thing I am certain about is that in an emergency people will be on their own for a while and won't exactly be reaching out to "older people" to check in on them. For that reason, I've been studying up on how to prepare just in case and believe every older woman living alone should take time to prepare. Here's some things I've already done to prepare that you may want to replicate for your own preparedness effort: (1) Purchased flashlights for every room in my house. Candles are okay but could create a fire risk if there are gas issues. (2) Bought batteries and a lot of them. If you purchase the more expensive ones they will last longer. I personally have solar powered battery chargers... worth looking into. (3) Rotated my water storage every 6 months because even water can go bad. If you think the power may go out for some reason, you can fill up your bathtub. (4) Bought 3-4 boxes of large garbage bags. You might need to poop on a newspaper and store up refuse in black plastic bags. (5) Stocked dry goods and canned foods. Remember to automatically restock and remember the manual can opener. Also try to keep propane in stock for grilling. The MINIMUM goal is enough food for 72 hours for everyone in the family – including pets. (6) Made a list of key phone numbers written down and placed for easy access. Assume you might not have 911 or internet, and (7) Purchased a solar phone charger.

Sally (76)

A Day in the Life: Marilou, Age 70

8:00	Drank two cups of coffee; read CNN news online; checked Facebook and LinkedIn. Made a smoothie to take with me when walking dog. Fed the dog.
9:00	Walked the Dog; Cleaned up the kitchen; put last night's dinner dishes in the dishwasher; thawed chicken; vacuumed the front room.
10:00	Walked 1.5 miles.
11:00	Prepared chicken for crock pot for Fiesta Chicken (new recipe)! Worked at computer on university business; returned up to 10 emails.
12:00 Noon	Weeded garden, watered and pruned all plants on the top deck; Repotted some small succulents for gifts this weekend. Made a ham sandwich for lunch with pork and beans. Not very healthy but one of my favorites. Fed the dog.
1:00	Worked on university business; wrote out a required work plan for 2018-2019. Not due until June but didn't want to have it on my "to do" list.
2:00	Rode bike to beach with dog and husband; sat on park bench looking at the ocean. Nice.
3:00	Worked on the first draft for a presentation entitled "Executive Presence" for a school leadership conference in November.
4:00	Went to LA Fitness and swam 20 laps. Sat in sun to get my legs tanned. Visited with some friends.

A Day in the Life: Marilou, Age 70

5:00	Went to Pacific City to use my $50 coupon for Tommy Bahama. Bought a new swim suit. Lost my validated parking ticked and had to plead with the attendant to let me out of $6.00
6:00	Walked the dog, checked the Fiesta Chicken; had a glass of wine and read for about 30 minutes.
7:00	Turned on CNN; ate the Fiesta chicken with my husband (yum yum) and had a glass of wine!
8:00	Watched recording of Westworld with my husband and treated myself to another glass of wine.
9:00	Called my son to see if all is good; Straightened up house from the day. Watched a movie on my IPad.
10:30	Walked the dog again. Sick dog that needs to go out a lot. Fed dog and then went immediately to bed; exhausted. Fell right asleep.
12:00	Woke up with horrible heartburn. Took a pill. Last time for Fiesta Chicken dinner!

ﺤ

LOSING THE SPANX

Most of the time I don't think about age. I live in a cup of reality a few days behind and a few days ahead. Of course, I have to plan some things for my business commitments several months ahead, but for the most part, I don't do much planning in my personal life. I just experience it and watch it unfold. Maybe that could be called denial, but I consider it freedom. For most of my life, I had to strategize, plan, compromise, and follow the rules of some employer. I always tried to shape my workplace into something great, but I continued to meet someone else's expectations and agendas. Now the only one who has an agenda for me is my family, which I gladly succumb to.

I also have the opportunity to be spontaneous. If I want to get up late, or go to bed late, I do that. If I want to go to Costco, I do that. If I want to garden, I do that. I eat when I want too, not at appointed times. I exercise by doing physical things around our property and aerobic gardening. I take a hand full of supplements every day and some before bed - it has made a huge difference in my health. My blood work is ideal according to the doctor, and my blood pressure is low. I gave up drinking all soft drinks about six years ago, which has made a huge improvement in my health. I still imbibe in alcohol periodically and will eat fast food occasionally when I want - Rubios' and Chipotle are my destinations of choice.

Patricia (69)

UP CLOSE and PERSONAL

Susan, Age 69

I arrive at Susan's home surrounded by the aroma of something cooking. Susan tells me she is cooking a Bolognese sauce for dinner. She also shares she plans to have her sauce with Zucchini noodles and serve her husband's over gluten free pasta. Susan reminds me she and her husband watch what they eat, trying to be healthy. At first glance, Susan looks a little sweaty and worked over, no doubt to her just finishing 18 holes of golf. She adds, I'll be showering after you leave. Truthfully, she looks beautiful, her hair fluffed and cheeks flushed. Looking around the house I begin to sense that Susan's priorities are her husband and family. There are many professional photographs of family members hanging everywhere.

She turns the burner to simmer on the Bolognese sauce and we take a seat at the table off the kitchen. I am pleased to be here and feel very comfortable with Susan. She has welcomed me into her home and made me want to stay longer than I anticipated, asking me to stay for dinner. Thank you, Susan, for your willingness and contribution to helping us pursue our sister to sister project. You are an inspiration to me and many more women looking for an enriched and happy life after 60.

Can you share anything you did when younger you believe has contributed to your good health today?

When I was younger? Probably not, because my mother always had us eat all our food on our plates. I became obese when I was younger. I was a size eight, then size 10. Then I was a size 20. When all my girl-friends were starting to date, I asked my brother's girlfriend, who was a young model doing little jobs, very pretty and in good shape, how I could lose my weight. She put me on an exercise program; you know the type... the good old touch your toes and then sideways and finally sit ups. At the time I lived on a third-floor tenement. I walked through all the floors throughout the tenement and of course she took me off sweets and potatoes. That was in April. In September, when I went back to school, I was down to a size 12 from a size 20. Nobody knew who I was. From that experience, and from then on, I always tried and continue today to be careful of what I eat.

That's a great story.

Well to qualify I was a kid then so I didn't follow it religiously, but I did take care of myself. I think today I take better care of myself now than when I was younger.

What kind of activities are you currently doing that influence your health today?

I walk. I didn't walk much back when I was heavy. I walk every morning. I just did something for myself I've always wanted to do and signed up all on my own. I joined a yoga class and I'm so excited. I said to my daughter, *I wish I could go again tonight but I need to learn how to do it first.* I know the first class is just learning terms and different kinds of breathing and all that, but I'm really excited about yoga. I think it's going to help with stretching and all that for me.

Do you have any special advice for women regarding being healthy as we grow older?

I can't say whether I follow it as an art, but I would advise women to stay away from sugar. Oh, those refined processed foods and alcohol, which we all know are very hard for us ladies to cut back on because we all love our cocktails. I would tell women to just be happy. Being happy is the key to staying healthy.

Would you describe any barriers you are currently experiencing with your health and share how you're addressing those challenges?

Well, I have back issues and my back is really bothering me. That was one of the reasons why I wanted to try yoga. I want to learn how to keep my body in a fluid motion stretching.

Can you describe how you feel about any changes in your body and how you are dealing with those changes?

My body is, for the first time, in a long time, feeling fat and old. It's happening on the midriff area. This change is bothering me terribly. I'm trying to learn that I'm going to be 70 and I can't have that thin flat stomach that I had 20 years ago. The flat stomach is just not going to happen again for probably 90 percent of us.

Yes, we've all got those Spanx. Can you give us one of your secrets for how a woman can have a positive personal appearance?

I'm going to be 70 and I don't look like I'm going to be 70 at all. I'm told people are very surprised and they think I'm turning 60. I know it's genetic, but also, I think it's because I've lived a very happy life. I have a great husband who has given me a good life. I don't have a lot of stress. I try to keep stress away from myself. I try not to worry because I think that's when people's bodies break down, when they react to the stress. So, I try not to get stressed. I try not to worry. When I go to sleep at night, I go to sleep very happy. I try to get eight to nine hours of sleep.

That's good advice. On another note, can you describe a recent time in your life that made you feel beautiful and young again?

That made me feel beautiful? Oh, yes, I was in a fashion show recently. They took photos and everything. It was a local show and I loved every minute of it. So, yes, I felt beautiful again, like when I was younger.

What spiritual areas, if you don't mind sharing, guide you through this phase of your life?

I truly believe in God. I feel as though when I speak to him, he guides me, and he answers. He answers a lot of my requests, but I always try to make sure I tell him to please have a good day himself. I don't like to always ask him for things. I like to tell him to do well. I think, if I didn't believe in God that I'd be empty on the inside. I don't go to church as often as I should. I don't feel the need to go every week because I feel God is with us all the time. We can speak to him wherever we are. When there's been a predicament in our family, I felt I needed to be truer to him.

For example, I went to church every single Sunday and prayed for my son in-law not to lose his job. He never did. I felt as though God listened. I guess that might be shallow to pray for that sort of thing. He and people would say, "*You mean you go to church because you think if you pray to God that God's going to save everything?*" I remember this person being very rude about it and I said, *I do. I do believe that.* I think if you don't have that faith, what is there to have? I mean, that's what we all do. We all prayed for these soccer players trapped in the cave, didn't we? It wasn't looking good. I think the world got together and prayed, everyone worked hard at praying, and all the soccer players got out.

Do you have any activities that help you regularly maintain your spiritual balance besides church and prayer?

I'd be disappointed in myself if I don't mention that this is something I love that gives me balance. I love to read. I love, love to read. I read every day. When my husband leaves for work in the morning, I say goodbye. I make myself a cup of coffee. I put the timer on for an hour and I sit and read for one hour. I don't answer the phone, but I look at it to make sure it's not an emergency. I read for my hour and it's awesome. I think that's important. You have that one hour to yourself and it's just yours; it's your power.

How would you define the word wealth?

Well, to me it means love. I have a very loving family. I think if every-thing was taken away from me monetary wise, I don't think it would matter because of the love we have.

You're being quite honest. On another note, just for fun… many women have a secret stash of cash on hand for whatever reason. Do you?

I have a secret stash of cash. And why? Well, it makes me feel inde-pendent to my husband whether it be a $20 bill or $100 bill. It's mine. I don't work anymore. I get the money from my husband obviously, but sometimes he doesn't know that I have a little extra hanging around.

Thanks for sharing that secret. Do you have any advice to give other women about saving or spending their money?

I probably can't share because I don't do that well with that. Give me a dollar, I'm going to spend that dollar. I have a daughter that does the same thing. I'm able to save enough money to buy those extra Christmas presents. I've stashed $30 or $40 away here and there, but I don't have any advice.

Can you share out of the ordinary anything you do to keep your mind thriving?

I do *Words with Friends* because keeping my mind active is a big concern for me. Sometimes I feel like I am getting very forgetful. You know, like, sometimes I ask, *Where am I?* Or *What side of the envelope do I put the stamp on?* Of course I know you put the stamp in the upper right corner. I do everything I can to keep my mind active. Playing Words with Friends is one way for me to keep my mind going.

What do you do now for fun? What, what kinds of things light up your life?

One thing that brings me joy, is spending time with my daughters and grandchildren. That's what makes me the happiest in life now.

What do you fear most about getting old and how do you address that fear?

I fear aging almost every day and I should not do this. I guess this contradicts what I say about not worrying, but I know that my time is short. I know there's going to be a grandchild that gets married and that bothers me that I might not be here. It brings tears to my eyes. I don't want to be that grandmother being wheeled in a wheelchair during the wedding. I want to be able to walk in as I am right now. I don't like getting old at all. I'm glad I'm here, you know. There's no alternative except not being here.

Now that you know what 70 almost looks and feels like, what advice would you give women approaching their 60s?

Oh, gosh. Just eat well and exercise. Enjoy life and be happy. Be happy. If you find yourself in a situation, you can always start over or you can erase what's happened and just move on. My advice is to not look back because the future is all there is left. You've already lived the past, so, just erase it and move on. I look forward to what the other women you are interviewing have to say.

SHABBY TO CHIC

My home is comfortable, inviting and unique. It pleases me. After all, I am the only one who lives here every day. I've never made a purchase for my home before asking myself if the item could be made or rehabbed from a second-hand shop. I've bought bedroom sets and kitchen tables but not without having a vision before purchasing them. I would always contemplate whether these items could withstand a facelift such as changing them with a bit of chalk paint or decoupage to enhance their look. My home is a work in progress as I am always involved in ongoing projects. I get creative satisfaction and instant gratification from all my hands-on projects. I recall a male friend who lived in an incredible home filled with priceless antiques, ultimate furnishings and designer labels stamped all over his décor. He gave me a compliment that made me both quiver and cringe when he said, "Beth your home... your home it's rather homespun." As I look back on this moment, I must have been low on confidence as I became ashamed and embarrassed of my decorating, most which I created with my own two hands. Almost 25 years has passed since hearing this message. Thankfully, today my creativity is still alive and blooming. My friends and visitors are always intrigued by my creativity and how I have put together rooms, decks, patios and party areas. Instead of hearing the word "Homespun" I receive compliments full of encouragement that I should market my talents. People offer praise for my uniqueness to put myself out there and be different. Finally, after 25 years I've reached a point in my life I can honestly be confident and secure in how and what I choose to create. In a way I'm thankful to this man's subtle insult. Not only did he get my creative juices flowing all these years, but he helped me find my individuality. I may be a little bit homespun but even more pleased that it's all my own spinning!

Beth (60)

SEVEN DAYS WITHOUT WINE
MAKES ONE **WEAK.**

A Day in the Life: Judy, Age 77

6:30	Woke up and read daily devotions
7:00	Fed dog, took her outside, made smoothies, drank smoothie, cup of coffee, read paper.
8:00	Straightened kitchen, made bed, walked 15 minutes, talked on phone to son.
9:00	Canned two batches of jam (new recipe). Very good.
10:30	Took dog outside.
11:00	Went to dental appointment.
12:00 Noon	Fixed lunch for husband and self.
1:00	Started planning about what to fix for dinner. Got meat out of freezer.
2:00	Watched the five on Fox.
3:00	Walked 15 minutes.
4:00	Sewed on baby quilts I'm making for unwed mothers.
5:00	Made and ate dinner.
6:00	Cleaned up kitchen.
7:00	Watered plants on porch and tended to plants. Sat outside on the swing and watched traffic.
8:00	Worked on quilts while watching TV and put a load of clothes into the washer.
9:00	Folded and put away clothes while the commercials were on.
10:00	Went to bed.
1:00	Woke up with leg cramps and had to go to the bathroom.
4:30	Woke up again with leg cramps and had to go to bathroom Slept until 7:00 AM.

❧

SCOTTY BEAM ME UP

As I grow older, I think a lot about memories. I have learned however that the past is the past and it's important for me personally to value each day. I read this book on mindfulness, very big on the West Coast, so I have been practicing being "mindful". So what can you do if you want to start practicing living in the moment? There are many strategies on the internet but most of them suggest a person should begin to train themselves by starting with something as simple as tooth brushing. I did just that and it really works. Try it. Next time you brush your teeth, ask yourself what does the toothpaste feel like as it touches your mouth, what does it taste like and how does the toothbrush feel in your hand? Concentrate on the entire activity of brushing your teeth; what does the water feel like, what do you see when you look in the mirror? If you can focus your brain for the entire time you are brushing your teeth, then yes... you have just learned to stay in the moment. After this exercise I tried it out with other activities and am beginning to enjoy life in the moment.

Louise (62)

❧

PASTRAMI ON RYE?

I now know and understand what it means to be part of the "sandwich generation." Having to worry and care for my mom, my grandson Bobbie and I guess I shouldn't leave out my own child and husband, has been quite a challenge. To think that in 19 years, I'll be my mom's age. I am really hoping that I use this opportunity of tremendous care giving to learn from these experiences, so I can make it easier on my kids.

Carolyn (63)

UP CLOSE and PERSONAL

Shelly, Age 72

I meet Shelly at a Starbucks halfway between her home and mine due to the large distance between us geographically. Shelly is a dignified looking woman with a strong presence. She looks a lot younger than her age and has a shapely figure. She is wearing a running outfit, a pony tail in her hair and a watch that looked as if it could launch a missile. I've only known Shelly for a few years and have admired her work in retirement. She's written some published articles about emotional intelligence in the workplace. As a retired chief executive officer of a transportation company, Shelly shared she doesn't miss the work at all but misses physically going to an organization every day. "Working in a large organization was like having another family," she said. "I miss my coworkers, the tech people and most of all my secretary. Not having a secretary in retirement is the worst," she complained. We stand in line to order our coffee and she doesn't miss a Starbuck's beat, ordering a Caramel Cocoa Cluster Frappuccino. I am prepared to pay for both our drinks, but she insists on paying for her own. We choose a seat in the corner of Starbucks and engage in some small talk before turning on the recorder for our interview. She seems happy to share her story, answering the questions with what seems like pure glee. Shelly is a fast talker and many times I have to ask her to repeat herself. I sense her mind is working overtime; she answers a question without hesitation always looking up to the right corner of the ceiling, appearing to search for more. I admire her directness, humor and honesty and her ability to share stories without any political or personal agenda. Shelly is the 'real deal' and I am grateful she allows me to include her in our book.

Can you share anything you did when you were younger that has contributed to your good health today?

Well, I used to swim a lot when I was younger, maybe that has had an effect on me today, because I really like to swim. I also played a lot of sports during my younger days when I was growing up and I think that's why I am in fairly good health today.

Is there something you wish you hadn't done in your younger years you are paying for now?

Smoking and having too much sex with so many different men before I was married. I heard that having a lot of sex over time can cause uterine cancer; I keep an eye on that with my doctor. Really, the smoking is the big difference. I can feel the effects of it on my body and lungs every day. I quit when I was around 50, but my God... *what was wrong with me?* I smoked almost two packs a day. My lungs are okay; at least when they do an x-ray on me. It says I am fine but I can feel the decline in my breathing. I wish I hadn't smoked.

Can you describe any activities you are currently doing that influence your health today?

Probably the walking, biking, swimming and just staying real active. I bought one of those Fitbit gadgets but it drove me crazy... 8,000 steps, get up and do another 10,000 steps for the day. I couldn't take it. I'm sort of an OCD person in the first place. I try to keep away from that stuff now. The Fitbit was like house arrest. I took it back to Best Buy and they gave me all my money back.

Do you have any special advice for women regarding maintaining good health as they grow older?

Yes, get up and spend most of your time being active. Sitting is not the way to stay young and healthy. I just read that most people over 60 spend over four hours sitting at their computers and another four watching television. That's not a lot of time for being active. Women, advice from me... get out of those chairs.

Would you describe any barriers you are currently experiencing with your health and how you are addressing those challenges to live a positive life?

Yes, on any given day, something hurts. Yesterday it was my left heel. I could hardly stand up. Today, it's my tooth. It pays not to perseverate on the stuff that hurts until it becomes unmanageable. Just yesterday someone asked me how I was, and I replied... *Well I woke up today and everything's working... so good, I'm good today.*

Can you describe any changes in your personal appearance or body, and share any thoughts about how you are dealing with them?

I hate them. I try not to live with it. I don't share this with anyone, but I had a face lift about ten years ago. It gave me another decade competing in the professional world. The majority of my friends all got them too. I always felt, and knew, there was a younger woman or man just waiting and ready to move into my job that I worked so hard to get. We can't be out there making the kind of money we are making, at this age, without trying to look a little younger or as I would like to call, "well rested." The plastic surgeon I used was well known for making women look natural and not doing the pinched, scary smile, facelifts you see on the movie stars. I took two weeks off from work. When I returned to work people commented that I looked well rested. I told them I went to Hawaii. As far as I know, no one, except my husband knew. After that facelift I got two promotions and almost doubled my salary.

Do you have any special advice for women regarding their personal appearance as they grow older?

When I would go into a department store the women working at the makeup counter would always grab me and give me a free make-up. I would walk out of there with over $200 of worthless products I believed would make my wrinkles go away. I got smarter along the way and began to realize these creams would not change the way I looked. So I started looking at fillers and cosmetic surgery. I believe if some-thing bothers you in your appearance and if you have the ability or money to fix it, then go for it. I get Botox and fillers all the time. They make me feel more attractive, and of course give me more confidence. I was really pretty in my younger years and I still think I look good. It takes money, time and the willingness to endure some pain on the back end. These Botox shots are nothing to sneeze at.

We all have special tricks of the trade to keep looking good. Would you mind sharing a few of your tricks?

Yes, I wash my face every day and then use prescription Retin A. I've been using it for 10 years and it has saved my face. I also drink a ton of water to flush out the toxins in my body. I do my own nails with a gel machine and I try to keep a thin waist. A thin waist makes clothes look better on a woman. I have to exercise every day to keep my waist looking small and that's not an easy thing. Also, I weigh myself every day; I have done this for the past 20 years. Remember, I am... a bit OCD... but I like to weigh around 125. So, if I get on the scale and it says 126 or 127 I don't eat much that day. I have been able to keep a steady weight as a result.

Can you describe a recent time in your life that made you felt beautiful and young again?

That's a hard one, let me think. Well it must have been the time, I think it was last year, I went out with my some of my girlfriends. I had on this black dress with high heels. These guys were giving us the "stare" and they were smiling, that sort of thing. I said to myself, *Hmmm... still got what it takes.*

What spiritual areas, if you don't mind sharing, guide you through this phase of your life?

I don't do the formal religion thing. I grew up a Lutheran and believed in God and all that. After a while, as I got older, I began to think of religion as merely being good to people and trying to help others. I keep a positive spirit in my mind and I don't do things that would hurt anyone. This is what I consider spiritual for me.

What kinds of activities do you participant in regularly to maintain a spiritual balance?

I try to be present when I am with people. That is a hard thing to do. I attended this workshop on being present a few years ago. I have tried to keep up with what I learned. Everyone in California is into the "being present" thing. It really works. Have you seen all these people walking around reading their cell phones? Ridiculous.

What does that mean for you, being present?

For me it means, that if someone is talking to me I listen to them and don't let my mind wander. I also try not to think about the past or forecast into the future too much. I try to keep a hard focus on the day that I am living. Make every minute count, that sort of thing.

When you hear the word "wealth" what does that mean to you?

Wealth... I think to me means family and friends. I have two children. It's important to me that they are all healthy and happy. I have had a wonderful career and keep busy with my life, but for me, it's all about my family. I am always thinking, are my kids happy, is my husband happy? I have been in a very competitive career, and you know what... those people don't mean a thing after all is said and done. When I look back on my life, the only thing that is important to me is family and friends.

When we talk about money or finances can you describe any strategies you use to keep up with the changing world of finance?

I have made a lot of money throughout my life, but you know what? I can't tell you anything about finances. Oh, don't get me wrong, I have a financial advisor who helps us and we save money, but I don't know anything about the stock market. I have always managed the finances in our family because I am type A. I worry about not paying the bills on time, that sort of thing. My husband could care less about the finances. He had his business and did well and managed his own finances with his auditors. We saved our money and spent it wisely. While I am only 72, I think we need to be cautious and not spend it all at once. Who knows how long we'll live and how long this money will last. Not me, that's for sure.

Many women have a Secret Stash of Cash on hand for whatever reason. Do you? If so, can you share why?

No need for a secret stash. However, my husband and I actually have a joint stash of cash hidden in our home that we could use in case of an emergency. You know, like in case the power grid goes down. We would have cash to use at the market for food and medicine, when the registers don't work.

What is the main thing you do in your life right now to save money?

Like I mentioned, we are very cautious with our savings and money right now. We aren't sure how long it will last. Hopefully we won't outlive our funds. I still do some outside consulting work and all that money goes into a special saving account for us, in case of a rainy day.

Do you have any advice for women about saving or spending money?

Yes, money doesn't buy happiness. I have found myself spending less and enjoying it more. I started downsizing our home this past year and taking all sorts of things to Goodwill that are just clutter. Believe me that was difficult. I would call it "weeding". I would say to my husband, I am going to weed that hall closet. I went to a house sale a few years back and was really depressed by what I saw when I went into one of the bedrooms. It looked like the couple who were having the estate sale [who I imagined were dead] slept in different bedrooms. Each bedroom had pairs of shoes arranged on the floor in front of the closets. Oh my… these people had together, I think around 200 pairs of shoes. It was as though they never threw any of them out. It was actually very disturbing and made a huge impression on me thinking about all the junk I was keeping. I didn't want to think about being dead and my children having to sell a 30-year-old dress I was saving.

Can you share anything you do to keep your mind thriving?

I work at this constantly, since it's one of my greatest fears of all for getting old. I take care of my face and figure but if my mind goes I don't know, it's a big worry. I tried doing that online program called Luminosity for a while and it seemed to work, especially with memory improvement, which I have not always been good at. Then I read on the internet that these online programs don't do anything to keep people's minds working. What I did read, however, was that doing different things and learning new things makes the cells in the brain work better and communicate better with one another. That's what I have been doing. I am learning to speak Spanish and loving it. One day I was in the bookstore and saw a practice book for the GED. I flipped through it and was shocked. I couldn't answer any of the math questions. I took advanced math in college and was quite good at the time, but over the years I didn't have much use for general math. So, I bought the damn book and retaught myself all those old skills that I was good at. You know… it felt good to be able to find the area of a triangle again. There was no reason for me to know this stuff now, but I was happy to have that skill set back in my life. Silly huh?

Some people say they have had difficult or stressful experiences, but have learned important lessons from them. Is that true for you?

Yes, I was fired from one of my executive positions toward the end of my career and was devastated. I thought I was done for and couldn't return. Fortunately, with a lot of networking and hard work I was able to get a new position within a month at a higher salary. What I learned was I was not listening very well to the people I was supervising. I should have known better. I always thought I was a good listener. In retrospect, my close friends shared I was the one doing all the talking. Listening is a very difficult skill to learn if you're the one who needs to do all the talking, which was my case. Now I try to listen before jumping into a conversation with my ideas... If I hear myself saying the phrase, *yes but...* then I know I'm not listening. That was a real wake up call for me and has helped me be wiser in my older years.

You are married. Can you share the secret to a happy relationship?

I have been married for over 50 years, and I always get a good laugh from people when I finish this sentence with... *to the same man.* I believe the secret to a happy marriage is trying not to make one another into a person that they are not. For example, I love my husband but he's not that social. I am very social. I tried to push that on him, he was just miserable. I didn't know it was bothering him until he said he couldn't stand it any longer. He said he tried but that he just likes to be with a few people, not out in all these social groups which I love. So we compromise. It was hard at first but worth it in the long run. So, yes, don't try to change the one you're with because it won't work out over the long run. Also the two of us retired within three months of one another and after we cleaned out all the closets, straightened up the garage, remodeled our kitchen and took three major vacations we sat down and looked at one another. *Now what do we do,* we asked ourselves? It seemed like work for us was very fulfilling. Now that we didn't have work to fill our days we were stuck; stuck with one another in this house. We needed to do some real soul searching and ask ourselves what we wanted to do with the rest of our lives. You can only travel so much, and besides, while I love to travel, it's very difficult and expensive. Well back to the soul searching. We both decided we needed to have something to share with one another. In addition, we both needed something of our own to enjoy. I decided to open up a small consulting business which is very rewarding. We both took up hiking, something I had no time for when working. We really like to hike together and visit different trails to explore. Things are better now…but one thing I would advise people is to think about a plan to walk into before actually retiring. Don't think that travel and remodeling a house will satisfy all your needs especially if you have been in high impact careers as we both were. I felt like I was getting off the treadmill and spinning out of control. Those were some tough times for us during our first few years of retirement.

What have you learned about living a happy and successful life today that you didn't know when you were twenty or thirty?

Take time to be present in the day. I never did that when I was younger and the days just went by so fast, and here I am in my 70s. I wish I had taken more time to absorb and enjoy each day.

As you look back over your life, do you recall any turning points that set you on a different course in your life?

I guess I have a fairly big ego because I was taking on too many projects for little return in my early 60s. I was doing this because I wanted to be noticed and considered a "player" in my field. I was chairing every committee, volunteering for every nonprofit, serving on boards, that sort of thing. One night I couldn't fall asleep and kept worrying about having to drive to Ventura on a Friday night to chair a large community event. I didn't want to take the drive and then spend the time and energy on this event. So, the next morning I woke up and said, *That's it. This is my last event for this organization.* I informed the key players I would be resigning. I still attend their functions but not as the chairperson. What a relief it was getting that off my plate. That was a real turning point for me. I learned I had to keep my ego in check and learn to say "no" to all the stuff that was coming my way. I don't need to be the center of attention, and you know what, it's a lot more fun in the long run. This was a big 'ah ha' for me and has served me well in my later years. I'm pretty good at managing my time now and don't want anyone to take power over that. My time is more precious than money.

What do you fear most about getting old and how do you address that fear?

I fear getting disabled and not being able to be independent. I am a very independent woman and would dread having to depend on someone to get my meals, bathe me, that sort of thing. I cross my fingers and try to stay healthy. I pay particular attention when I am walking so that I don't trip and fall. I've had a lot of my friends fall and break a leg or hip. When I walk I try to stay in the zone and make sure of what's in front of me when walking. Also I am really cautious about stepping off of curbs, any curb for that matter.

What would you say are the major values or principles you live by?

I am really disturbed right now about the division in our country and am trying to stay involved politically with some different diversity groups. I am an active LGBT supporter and involved in some of their associations as an advocate for their cause. I feel bad for African Americans right now in our country and never thought their lives could be so bad. I was oblivious to what they may be experiencing and how they feel and how they are profiled. My values are about equality. Equity for all races, for women, for gay and lesbians, for everyone. I live and breathe that every day. I try to infuse some positive dialog into the conversation when these issues come up. I feel so strongly about the shift in American politics right now that I am considering running for some small local office in our town. I don't know, I am just thinking about it. I am on a committee to help register voters for the midterms this fall so I'll see how that goes. But my values... respect and dignity for every living soul on this planet. That's what wakes me up in the morning and gives me purpose. It always has.

What advice would you give women a decade before you, now that you know what 70 feels like?

I could write a book, but I guess you're doing that. Okay, eat right, don't drink too much alcohol, establish some girlfriends to hang out with, get a dog, exercise every day and be present. Life is short. Oh, yes, and learn to say no if you have a big ego and think you are pretty special. Don't forget to take care of your face with sunscreen. Save your money but don't be a miser and try to do new and different things in your life. Most importantly, take good care of your family and friends. Thanks for listening. This has actually been fun for me. I can't wait to read the book.

OLIVE BRANCH

There are a few people in my life I have had to sever my relationships with. I felt the decision to do so was the best thing for myself and family. Now so much time has passed and I think about reconnecting with these people. Sadly they are related to me. I want to try to reconnect before it becomes too late for any of us. However, I am a coward. I am so afraid of being rejected should I contact any of them. It's not that I feel I deserve to have their attention but that they won't desire mine. I will never know until I try. So what will hurt more… being rejected or being protected? Time is moving faster and faster the older I become. I need to decide whether to reach or retreat before it is too late. Something tells me to take a chance and slowly I will find some peace either way. I've never been a risk taker but I'm about to become one soon!

Marie (65)

My deal. No Sue, it's Dottie's Deal. No Joan, I just dealt. You did? So who just shuffled the cards? Me. Wait. What? Linda, you shuffled? Yes, so it's my partner's deal. So who cuts the deck? OMG! Here give them to me. I will shuffle, cut and deal!...

...Who's on First?

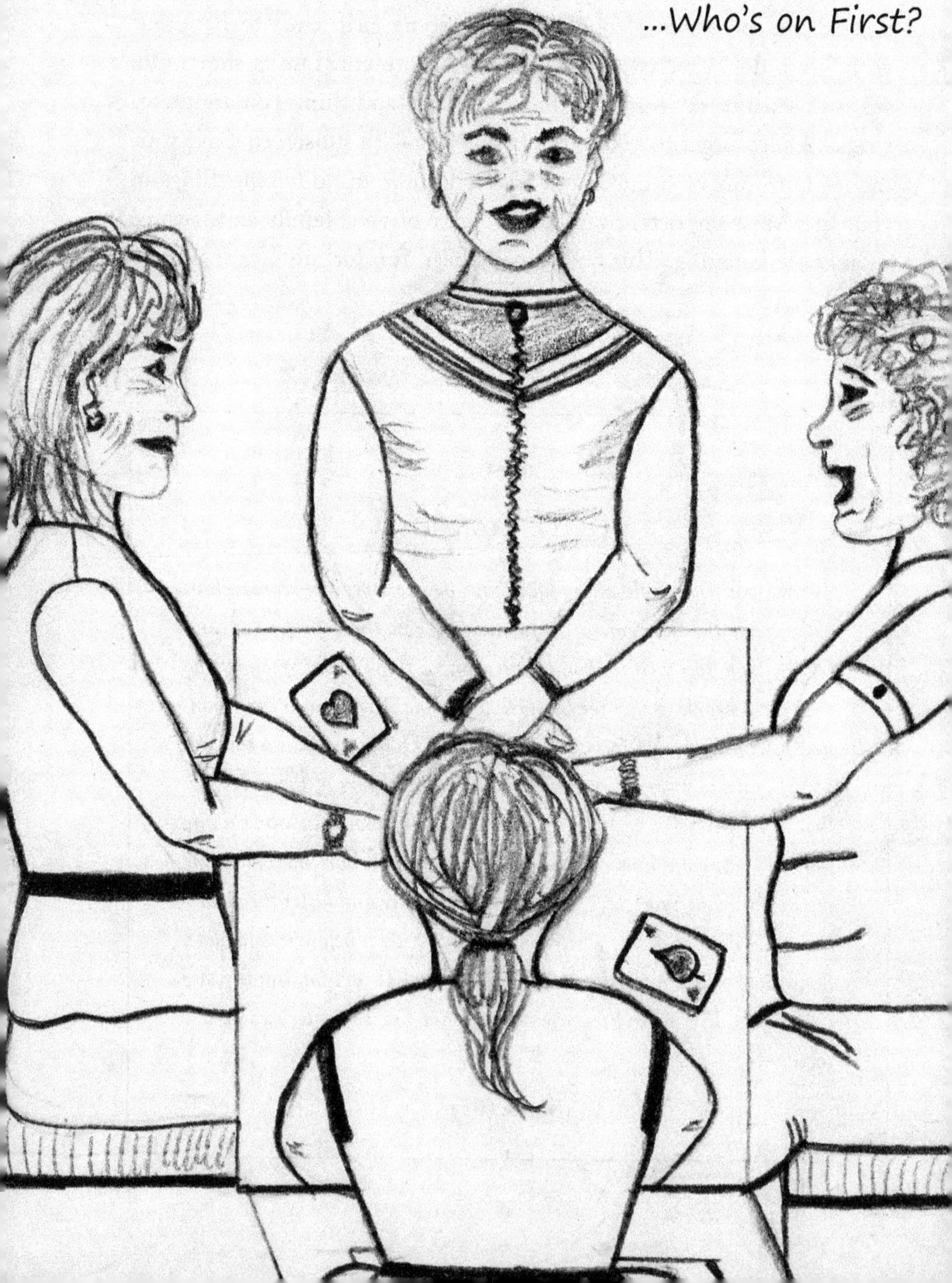

A Day in the Life: Susan, Age 66

6:00	Woke up before the alarm clock which was set for 7:00. Waited in bed until I was sure my husband had the coffee brewing.
6:15	Brushed teeth took daily thyroid supplement and assorted vitamins to keep heart and joints moving smoothly ☺
6:30	Took seat at kitchen counter with lap top, cell phone and coffee. Sun is shining today and the river is sparkling! TV was tuned into channel 4 (WBZ) to catch the local news.
6:45	First on my to-do list was to wish my grandson a Happy 17th Birthday...then spent the next hour checking text messages, email, bank statements, paying bills, reading news feeds and managing my Airbnb account (Need to communicate with up-coming guests, check all vacant nights to make sure they are priced right).
7:45	Off the bar stool with second cup of coffee in hand and on to laundry and some light clean up in our guest room (Friends stayed with us 4 nights this week) and a shower.
9:00	All showered and back to kitchen counter for breakfast and a little FOX news.
9:30	Unfortunately, no work-out today. Instead, I'm off to pick up a friend to attend another friend's mom's funeral service. Our greatest generation is slowly being replaced by our generation. We have become them!
12:00	You know what they say about all work and no play... So, now time for some golf! Met my husband and 2 friends for a round of golf. We got a big surprise on the 10th hole when our good friend, met us on the fairway with cocktails.

A Day in the Life: Susan, Age 66

4:30	Finished golf, tallied score, grimaced about how my game is in a slump and headed home. On way home chatted with my daughter about the trials and tribulations of her day and her family's plans for the weekend.
5:00	Quick check of email, sent an Airbnb message, put in a load of laundry, washed up and got ready to go to the Grog to meet friends for an early dinner and yes, more drinks!
6:30	Nice dinner at Grog...conversation was very lively and a bit confrontational when the subject of the Patriots came up. Will they be as good as previous years???
9:30	Got home, put laundry in dryer, quickly got into pajamas and tuned in my recording of Nashville. I hope Avery doesn't fall for the new girl in the band, Alannah ☹
10:30	Read for 15 minutes and realized eyelids were very heavy so shut the lights out. Great Day...Good Night!

ZERO TOLERANCE

I love throw rugs. I love how they jazz up a house and add color and diversity to a room. I loved them so much until I slipped on one and broke my hip. I was in the hospital for three days, had two surgeries and still have pain two years later. Ladies... take it from me. Lose the throw rugs. Any rugs you purchase should have a nonslip bottom on them. It's just not worth the risk in my humble opinion.

Patty (60)

EVERY GOOD BOY DOES FINE

If you took music lessons like me when you were a kid, you probably recall the phrase Every Good Boy Does Fine to help you remember the names of the lines on a music scale. I personally like mnemonics as a tool to help me remember facts or a large amount of information. For me it can be a song, rhyme, image, or a simple phrase to help me remember a list of facts in a certain order. In addition to using this strategy to help me remember simple things, I have a similar trick I use when I think my memory is starting to fail. You know the feeling... you walk into a room and can't remember why you are there. I have a game I play that (for me) really works. When I'm taking a long drive or working around the house I say to myself, "Think of a fruit or vegetable that begins with every letter of the alphabet. Then I start... Apple, Beets, Corn, etc. At the end of the alphabet I start over to see if I can remember what my list was. I do this 3 or 4 times to strengthen my memory. This little exercise has been essential for me and a big factor for why I think my memory still works. By the way I even do this when I am waiting in the medical office waiting for my latest medical procedure. It calms me down for some reason and keeps me from being nervous. Try it, you'll like it! Apple, Beets, Corn, Dates, Eggplant, Fig, Grapes, Huckleberry, Iceberg Lettuce, Jicama, Kale, Lime, Mango, Nectarine, Okra, Plum, Quince, Raspberry, Strawberry, Tomato, Ugli Fruit, Vanilla Bean, Watermelon, Xigua, Yams, Zucchini.

Roberta (72)

⸎

FOUNTAIN OF YOUTH

I have worked every day since turning 16 and am still working. I can honestly say I have enjoyed every job I've ever had. I don't wait for the joy to come to me, I go after it. I choose work that is creative and interesting, but mostly I surround myself with people who are both competent and fun to work with. Collaborating and learning with a team of enthusiastic people who are excited about creating new programs and solutions is extremely energizing. Learning together is the fountain of youth! I plan to work for as long as I can. I love the freedom of having financial independence and feeling like I am still part of the universe. Don't count me out just yet!

Maxine (78)

〰

SAY IT LOUD AND I'M PROUD

Before I retired, I joined the cancer crowd and had radical breast surgery in November 2010. One of the things I've learned to do is not compare myself to my youthful days. I am one of three girls and both my sisters had long hair, not me. Both of my sisters had small breasts, not me. I was very uncomfortable with both but now I'm proud to say I could possibly go 2-3 days without combing or brushing my hair and no one would notice. I'm also finding out that people do not notice I do not have breasts so I feel good taking my shower, washing my hair and say, that's it. My prosthetics (boobs and bras) are in the room in a drawer. I'm proud to be able to say I'm fat, fabulous, flat and almost bald.

Margie (68)

UP CLOSE and PERSONAL

Anna, Age 73

I arrive at Anna's house at 5:30 PM. When I enter her home I gasp at how incredibly elegant it is, mostly decorated with white silver, gold, and shades of gray. The rooms are spacious with large windows adorned with silver swags puddled on the floor. Her home is cool, calm, and peaceful. Anna's daughter is busy heating some appetizers for us and offers me a glass of wine. I choose red. It just fits the mood. We sit outside in a covered porch with beautiful plants, creative lighting fixtures and a bubbly water fountain. I feel like I am in the lobby of an elegant spa waiting to hear my name called. So, now try and picture Anne Margaret in Bye Bye Birdie; red hair flipped up at the ends and poofed on top; a gorgeous figure with a white strappy dress cinched at the waist, with a full skirt. That is Anna tonight, at 73, with matching pumps to go with her dress. Her bronze freckles are spattered across her nose and shoulders. At the moment, I feel like a preppy beast next to her in my khaki skirt, button down dress shirt and flip flops, but Anna smiles as her daughter delivers an enormous tray of fruit, cheese, and hot appetizers. I am so relaxed being here and can't wait to learn of Anna's rituals that have gotten her this far in life. I believe I am in the presence of a woman who is as beautiful on the outside as on the inside. Cheers to you, Anna, and thank you with all my heart.

I'm hoping you can share anything you did when you were younger that you believe has contributed to your good health today.

Well, I must say I was never a sun lover. I always tried to stay out of the sun but that wasn't because I didn't like the sun. It was because the sun was always bothering my eyes. So I sort of stayed on the good side of the sun. I ate fruit and fresh vegetables, which my mother always made. Overall, my mother made us have good eating habits. And I always exercised. I was very active, always very active.

Is there anything you did when you were younger that you might be paying for today?

On my health? No, because I think I pretty much stayed active and was always concerned that as I aged I needed to take care of my health. It's always been a priority of mine.

Can you describe any activities you are currently doing that you feel influence your health today?

Well, I still run. But not as far as I used to. I can run probably four miles. I work out at the gym three days a week—Pilates for one class, in another class muscle conditioning. The other class is more like an aerobics class. In between I do a run.

Four miles, that's a lot. How many days a week do you think you do that?

I don't do it as often because of time. Once, twice a week, but in between the walk and then running. So it's not always a four-mile run.

Do you have any special advice for other women regarding maintaining good health as they grow older?

Don't be afraid of stairs unless of course something has happened and you have problems walking. Don't avoid climbing stairs. I know so many women who hate going up the stairs when actually they could. They look for ways not to use the stairs and I think stairs are great because when you use them you don't even realize you are getting exercise. That's true because when you look at a lot of condos and apartments for people now, they're designed with the one bedroom on the first floor.

That's because people don't want to use the stairs. I love stairs. I have three sets of stairs in my house.

Do you keep track of your steps and things like that?

No, I just know how far I've gone and go up and down stairs each day.

Would you describe any health barriers, if any, you are currently experiencing and how are you addressing those challenges to live a positive life?

I think since I turned 73, I find the winters are a challenge. When I am home, I get tired at night and the winter days are much harder. Like about 4:00 P.M. whereas before I'd be going back out again but now I don't feel like doing that.

We get hard winters in New England. So, when you stay at home, are you comfortable with that?

When it's really cold, I'm pretty happy staying in. I'll do a lot of cooking to keep myself busy.

Can you describe how you feel about these changes in your personal appearance and share any thoughts on how you deal with these changes?

I guess you just do the best you can, to look the best you can. Well, of course I moisturize a lot. I condition my hair a lot. I think it's important, of course, being a hairstylist to look my best.

Are you still working?

Yes, I am still working. I work two days a week and Saturday and Wednesday if they need me. I own this salon with my daughter. We've had our salon about 11 years. We had to relocate due to a variety of factors. Before that, I worked in another salon since I was 20.

That's a long time. So you moisturize, you condition your hair. Any other things you can think of?

I'm not a big sweet eater and I don't eat a lot of meat.

Do you have any special advice for women regarding their personal appearance as they grow older?

You know, I think I do have some advice. I think that when some women hit a certain age they believe they have to dress as though they're 80 or 90 years old. I don't think they need to dress like that. I mean, I'm certainly not saying they should be wearing miniskirts and low-cut dresses or that sort of thing. What I see, which is pretty common for the people I know, is that when women get old they give up. I wish they knew that they don't have to dress like an old lady even though we are.

So give us an idea about you. What makes you feel good? What do you think is your style?

I think by now at this age you know your style. You know what works and what doesn't work for your body. I'm tiny, so naturally I'm not going to wear big bulky clothes. I think I found what works for me, and what looks best on me, and I stick with that. I don't try to wear things just because they are in fashion at the time. I don't try to dress with the latest fashion trends because I think they are mostly for the kids. When I was a kid, I wore them all, but now I am careful to not dress like an old lady. We have to dress with some thought. I don't want to say conservative because that's the last thing I think about myself when it comes to style, but just a little style, and keep away from dowdy. Maybe it's because I've been in the beauty business for so long, but I see so many women and I want to say to them, "You are making yourself look older." I think maybe it's because they feel uncomfortable. Oh and yes, and don't go to the make-up counter like Macy's.

Why?

That girl working the make-up counter is there to sell products, not to really help you. Yes, the only reason she is there is to sell you. She's not in the makeup business. Now on the other hand, I would tell women to go to someone who knows what they are doing and who is going to show you how to contour your face. Now, don't think I wear make-up every day and don't misunderstand me. I certainly do not get all made up when I'm running out the door and everything. But as an older woman, know how to contour your face. Apply some good make-up… don't be afraid of make-up. Don't be afraid of a little eye shadow or blush. I've always taken my clients, especially the ones in their eighties and given them some makeup advice and they love it. "Can I share a little blush on you?" I ask. They go home feeling beautiful and they are. And not everybody has to be a 10. I do this because I really care. I love woman, and love people.

So Anna, can you describe a recent time in your life that made you feel beautiful and young?

Let me think. Okay, yes. Whenever I am out with my husband, he tells me that I look good. You know, I mean, even though he knows I'm not 27 or 30 years old anymore. That makes me feel good.

I would like to talk a little bit about the topic of spiritual wealth. What spiritual areas, if you don't mind sharing with me, guide you through this phase of your life?

Just my belief in God. I have a lot of faith. When you see me walking around I am talking to God.

What are some of the activities you do to regularly maintain your spiritual balance?

I go to church every Sunday and I really like the holidays. I really enjoy Christmas, just the whole feeling of being close to God at that time.

When you hear the word wealth, what does that mean to you?

Listen, if you've got happiness and you've got a family that's wealth to me. It's always nice to have money and a lot of money is even nicer. Having a lot of love in my life is important to me. I have great women mentors in my life and I deal with a lot of women that are wonderful, wonderful women. So, I think that's what wealth means to me… wealth is just about people, my daughter and that's all the wealth I need.

You say you deal with a lot of women. Are they your clients?

They are my clients, my friends, my relatives. My sister-in-law, I've known since I was 16. She's very nice and we get along great. I never had any sisters. I had my friend Barbara who was 20 years older than me. I was very close with her. She was a great friend and great mentor to me in my life. I feel very lucky that I have had a lot of good strong woman, very strong women in my life. These were the type of women that were very caring and when things went bad in their lives they always seem to bounce back. I think I picked that up from them. You know, you have a lot of really, really low times in your life, but you just can't lie there and wallow in it. It doesn't make any sense and it's not that healthy. It doesn't help anybody else when you are in that state. You just have to get up and make things better if you can.

When we talk about money or finances, can you describe any strategies you use to keep up with the changing world?

Yes, you have to be looking ahead all the time. You have to be prepared for tomorrow. We can't just live for today. You have to learn how to save also. I would say it's critical to keep up with the future. In my business you have to keep up with what's happening with new hairstyles, that sort of thing. You just can't do what you did 30 years ago and then grow in this world. Everything is moving pretty fast. You need to keep up with what's going on. For example, I watch a lot of financial stations all the time. I'm not sure I understand all of it, but I'm trying to keep up.

How do you keep yourself familiar with the internet, social media and updates in technology?

I've kept up for what I need. I am on the computer a lot. I know a lot of things about using a computer, but a lot of it I'm finding too invasive now. A lot of it I don't really want to learn how to do. It's not that I can't do it, it's that I am not sure I want to do my banking and certain things financial on a computer. I just don't feel secure.

That's okay. You like to keep your privacy. So many women have what they call a secret stash of cash on hand for whatever reason. Do you?

Oh yeah, I always have a secret stash. Why? Because you should always have a secret stash. That is always one thing I do; absolutely.

What do you do with that?

Honestly, a lot of times when I have saved money, it will be because somebody needed the money and I would be able to help them. So, it's more for somebody else other than myself, like if an emergency came up or something that like.

What financial advice would you give women younger than you?

I would tell them to get themselves a nice financial advisor. Absolutely, go and do that. Get somebody you trust, because again, things are going fast.

What do you mean by things are going fast?

Well even with your finances, even your stocks shift. It's a real fast world out there right now and much faster than it was four years ago. Much, much faster.

Are you able to keep up with it?

Well, I am because I pay attention to the stock market. I'm still able to keep up. I think if I had to, I wouldn't have a problem getting out there and making good decisions. I feel secure, and I'm always thinking about different ways to make money. I'm always looking at property. That's a good thing.

Can you share anything out of the ordinary that you do to keep your mind thriving?

I think working at a job helps a lot. I keep up with the news by watching the financial stations and reading newspapers with current events. I love current events. I think exercising also helps mental health. Exercising cleanses your mind. You get that good energizing feeling after you run, it always kicks in. Yeah.

Are you good about communicating with friends and family members who may not live nearby?

Yes, I do but not as much as I'd like to. I have so many clients that give me a lot of information and I often participate in social media by emailing.

You're married. If possible can you share the secret to your happy marriage?

I've been married for 67 years. The secret for us? I guess it's just having a love for each other even though we know everything about each other isn't perfect. We always manage to get over it and live a happy life.

What would you say about living a happy and successful life that you didn't know when you were younger?

I think I now know there are things you can't change. What is going to be, is going to be. I think when I was younger I tried to change things. Like people think you can change a person after you get married, change the person to be something you want them to be. Now I realize I can chill. Now I realize I can just relax and enjoy life.

What types of things did you try to change when you were younger?

Well, thinking about marriage, and thinking you could try to change people. Everybody is different. When you are younger, you think to yourself that you can change someone for the better. I've always tried to help people, but helping the person and changing them are two different things.

So, let me ask you this, as you look back over your life, do you see any turning points that set you on a different track?

I always knew that I was going to have a business even when my children were young. I had my son when I was 19 but I always wanted to advance myself for them, so, they could grow. I always wanted a business someday, and I think I always had that in my head.

What do you do for fun now? You're not retired, you're still working. In other words, what makes you happy right now?

I am quite easy to please. A walk on the beach, I love it. A vacation. I love sitting on my deck having a glass of wine.

So you're pretty content. You enjoy things as they come?

Yes. I think I am content now because I don't have that extreme drive. I am content because I don't feel that extreme motivation to doing something all the time, like when I was younger.

When did you stop feeling that drive?

I didn't stop altogether. What I should say is that I'm more relaxed now about it and about accomplishing things. I never stop thinking about what else could I do, but it's not as intensive as it used to be.

Do you ever get the feeling that if you're not doing something, you're wasting your time?

I do. So, if I'm just sitting, I will be looking around. If I were sitting here right now alone I would be thinking I have to attend to the grass and I have to get the gardening done.

What do you fear most about getting old and how do you address that fear?

You know what? I see so much fear in people about this. Especially with my clients that have gotten older. I think the people who make it, keep healthy and thrive. They don't think about getting old. You just can't dwell on it. You can't get scared about it. You're getting older, that's it. When your time comes, it comes. One of my clients was telling me just this month, "When the time comes your feet are going to take you there." The woman told me her belief in the morning and that very night she died on the dance floor. And she died dancing. That's a true story. She must have sensed something as I look back on that day.

How old was she?

She was about 75. I don't dwell on it. I really don't. I don't know what's going to happen. It's going to happen. I'm just hoping that I don't have to just lie there and be in pain. I hope I have this massive coronary and just go.

What would you say are the major values or principles that you live by?

I love my family and try to help my family. Definitely. It's very important to me.

Finally, my last question. I'm 61 you're 73. What would you tell my generation to prepare for when they reach their 70s?

All you should do is just keep going and do what you're doing. Don't give up, don't give in to your aches and pains and just keep going. And don't start dressing like you're 90 years old!

THE WIZARD OF OZ

Be proud of getting older because along with age comes wisdom. Use your wisdom and knowledge for good. Build others up rather than tearing them down, and you will never be alone. Seek the beauty and wonder in everything! Savor the good as well as the bad. Life is fleeting, and eternity is forever. You will be rewarded for all the good things you have done.

Rebecca (77)

THE YOUNG AND THE RESTLESS

Our parents' life styles were expected to decline. They generally didn't walk around the block every day or use a stationary treadmill or swim or hike and so their limbs atrophied. I believe as a result we still have those mental models we observed in our parents and that the symptoms of what we define as old age begin at 50, settle in at 60 and by 70, if we are still alive we are discussing our head stone.

However, new aging definitions in the latter part of the 20th and 21st century have emerged. We see several examples of people over 60 identified in magazine articles doing more than what we expect older people to be able to do. Our baby boomer generation goes to the gym for routine exercise, practices yoga for flexibility, and finds ways to add healthy supplements or food to their bodies. Technology advances in medicine have also extended our time and quality of life. While the domino effect of taking so many pills for depression, aches and pains, and inflammation may eventually catch up with us in unexpected ways, the data shows that the quality of life is extended by sometimes 35% with life expectancy now generally between 80 and 90 years of age in the twenty-first century. Age is just an attitude and representative of what you create in your mind. I love to read stories about women doing spectacular things in their 60s and 70s. These women inspire me to say, "I feel like I am in my 40s or 50s, so I will continue to act like I am." Yes, I am concerned about dementia, but I believe keeping my mind active will delay this affliction; however, if Alzheimer's besets me, I anticipate there will be a cure or a treatment which will alleviate the symptoms of this disease. I believe I will live to 90 or more. My adoptive mother died at 91. She was active every day, never smoked, was stubborn, and ate healthy by sometimes feeding us vegetarian meals before it became popular. She was amazingly young even in her eighties and hung out with people twenty to thirty years younger that loved having her in their company. Her influence and continuing to read about the new definition of "being old" is what I do to remain young at heart as well as in body and spirit.

Duchess (70)

A Day in the Life: Marie, Age 67

7:00	Woke up. Made and drank 3-4 cups of coffee. Read newspaper and checked email.
8:00	Fed the dogs and took a shower.
9:00	Started a load of laundry and read materials for a school board meeting.
10:00	Attended a construction site meeting (we are building a new home).
11:00	Site meeting until 12:00.
Noon	Drove home and made and ate lunch..
1:00	Wrote an email to resubmit Chapters 1-3 for revisions for a doctoral student.
2:00	Met a friend and took a 4 mile walk in the woods with the dogs
3:00	Stopped at the market for groceries and drove home.
4:00	Practiced piano.
5:00	Finished laundry and worked on a meeting agenda; prepared dinner.
6:00	Ate dinner, drank wine and watched Rachel Maddow.
7:00	Watched Lawrence O'Donnell.
8:00	Cleaned up dinner dishes and read a novel.
9:00	Checked and answered emails – read internet news.
10:00 PM	Went to bed and back to reading the novel again until I fell asleep.

❦

WOMAN'S BEST FRIEND

Max is my best friend; don't know what I would do without him. He is with me from morning to night and I am really devoted to him as [I think] he is of me. We are inseparable. If I were to offer women any advice about getting older, I'd say get a dog if you can afford it and if you have time to care for it. If you like to travel, wait to get a dog as they do have a way of imposing on long travel plans. Many of my friends agree; we get too attached to our dogs and aren't that keen on leaving them for weeks on end in a kennel. Lord knows what happens to them while we are living it up on the cruise ship. I've heard cats are easier when leaving for periods of time. My dog is my lifeline. I live alone and when I wake up in the morning I like to talk and there's no one to talk to except for my dog who always listens intently. And when a slight mood of depression takes hold sometimes around 4 or 5 PM I play some games with my dog and feel happier immediately... my mood goes from pale to positive in a few minutes. Dogs can be a woman's best friend, and that's a real comfort for me as the days turn into weeks within the blink of an eye. I do worry though if something were to happen to me about who will take care of my dog. So make sure you follow up on that end of the friendship. My son has promised to take my dog should he outlive me... the dog that is.

Nancy (88)

Lord help the mister who comes between me and my sister and Lord help the sister who comes between me and my man.
SISTERS SISTERS... THROUGH ALL KINDS OF WEATHER WE STICK TOGETHER. THERE WERE NEVER SUCH DEVOTED SISTERS.

❦

POOPED OUT ON PERFECT

As a young career woman I was known as something of a perfectionist. A lot of people criticized me for this, but it seemed to work since I got job after job with higher pay. I always thought doing the best job at whatever I was involved in was important and attributed this trait to my career success. I once sent back an entire publication which cost our firm dearly because of a glaring typo on the front page of a newsletter. As I became older, I still have that edge to me but not so much. As I look back at trying to be "perfect" all the time, I think it was a lot of work and sometimes may have even distracted me from more import-ant things I could have been doing. Now I try to do my best with every-thing but more so in moderation. Everything doesn't have to be perfect. I have a new way of thinking now… it's called "Pretty Good".

Marjorie (65)

❦

NO THANKS, I'LL WALK

My advice to other women getting on in years… resist using a mobility aid until you really, really need one. Once you take residence on one, for whatever reason, you'll have a hard time turning back. The same goes for trying to talk your doctor into authorizing a Handicap park-ing permit. Don't do it. I'm not saying you should resist an aid if you are injured or really need one for medical reasons and your doctor has recommended it. Merely, I am recommending that we resist for as long as possible, if possible. My advice, take it or leave it but it works for me.

Susan (75)

❦

WASH, RINSE, REPEAT

I got sick and tired of forgetting simple things. Oddly, I did not attribute this to getting old but rather blamed multitasking, social media and the influx of new knowledge coming at me with record speed on the internet. I would meet someone new, get introduced and then grasp at straws to remember their name after hearing it uttered just a few seconds prior. That's when my friend told me her secret. She said when she wants to remember something she repeats it a few times right after hearing it. For example, when she is introduced to someone, she says their name two or three times in the conversation hoping to lodge it in her short-term memory. She also uses this strategy with new knowledge or something that her doctor has told her to do. Now I use this trick at least once a week or more to help me remember things that are important.

Beverly (64)

❦

A LITTLE DAB'LL DO YA

I recently read that maintaining a good level of Vitamin D is one of the cheapest and easiest ways to improve my health and life expectancy. And one of the quickest means to get that Vitamin D is to be outside in the sunlight. I try to go outside for at least 15-30 minutes a day even if it means just sitting outside for a little while on the grass in the sunlight. Not only is Vitamin D essential for bone health, but I also heard that taking Vitamin D impacts levels of depression and heart disease. For me personally, I think sunlight helps me feel happier and more positive about life. I'm not an expert but I highly recommend women try this simple method to improve and/or maintain their wellbeing.

Amber (80)

UP CLOSE and PERSONAL

Barb, Age 73

O n a Thursday morning, I meet up with Barb, age 73, at a Dunkin Donuts convenient for both of us. I arrive before her and become a bit uncomfortable because the place is so noisy. I am hoping I can hear every word she speaks. After a few minutes I see Barb approaching the coffee shop entrance in a comfortable knit top, shorts and sneakers. Her hair is stark white and is very becoming on her. She's a woman who can carry that shade of hair. Barb is spunky and happy. This morning we hug and I treat her to coffee without a muffin or doughnut. Barb has already had her breakfast. I imagine she's probably been up since 5:00 A.M. We take a seat in a nearby corner and begin to enjoy one another's company.

We talk about our latest golf outings on Fridays and how our league is doing. I've always been drawn to Barb because she reminds me of a very famous woman we have all seen on television, 'Mom' on the Golden Girls. She not only resembles her appearance, but she has that quick-witted sense of humor. Barb's voice is similar to Mom's, raspy and indirect with one difference, an extreme Boston accent. Barb is a true native to a suburb of Boston. How appropriate the two of us wanted to meet at Dunkin Donuts. We both feel at home and comfortable, a familiar place with good coffee. Barb is a kind, honest, and very sincere human being. There's something about her that wishes she were your very own guardian angel on your shoulder every day of your life. Stay special forever, Barb, and continue to spread your kindness. Thank you for brightening up my day with a good cup of Joe.

Thanks for meeting me today. Can you share anything you did when you were younger that has contributed to your health today?

I think the way we were bought up at home back in the day, like the fresh food we ate was critical. I believe I've been to McDonalds twice in my life, really, only twice in my life. We didn't do fast food with a lot of chemicals in them. My mother was big on that. One of my mother's friends had a farm and she used to bring us fresh eggs. We had a milkman who delivered fresh milk. I think that made a difference for me now that I am actually attuned to what tastes good as opposed to what everybody tells you should taste good. Looking back, I think that was important and was the way it was. I mean, my mother worked nights, my father worked days. We always had breakfast. We always had dinner together around the table. We always helped her cook, so we knew what she was preparing, whether we liked it or not. I think that made a difference.

Can you share anything you wish you hadn't done when you were young that you're paying for today?

I wish I hadn't quit music lessons. I took music lessons for a while as did my sisters, but I didn't want to take them anymore. I don't know why, but then all of a sudden, I say, *jeepers, why hadn't I followed through?* I wish I had followed through. I was playing violin and my sister played piano. I didn't want to do it anymore.

How long did you play your musical instrument?

I was going into high school. I didn't want to play an instrument anymore. I don't think at that age you understand what a basic understanding of reading music is and what to do with it and what you can do with it later in life. I didn't have my own instrument which was another thing. They only had violins for us to play. We would practice the violin at school and I didn't want to practice in front of a bunch of boys. That was then, but I wish I had stayed with music.

Can you tell me any activities you are currently doing out of the normal that influence your health today?

I don't consider what I do today out of the normal. I walk a lot and I swim. I have a pool in the backyard to swim. I swim like a swan and I love swimming. Today it was overcast and kind of cold and I didn't want to go out there and I said to myself, *For crying out loud, 10 minutes, go out there, swim around, come in and take a shower.*

And you did that? How many laps?

It's a small pool. So I swam five down, five back, let's call it ten laps. I used to teach swimming and I used to coach the Special Olympics for over 30 years. My brother has Down syndrome and that's how I got involved in coaching. I think also that my brother made a difference in how we played as kids. My mother worked at night and my father worked days so that someone could always be home with my brother to take care of him. We always played with one another rather than get shipped out to play in the neighborhood. We took care of one another.

Is there anything that you feel is a barrier that you're experiencing with your health now?

I'm very fortunate. I'm very healthy, I don't have any aches and pains.

What about any changes that you're witnessing?

The white hair is a big change for me but it doesn't bother me. The only thing that kind of bothers me, at times, on my face, are the wrinkles, but that's my fault. You know, when you were a young kid, did you put sunscreen on your face? I mean, they didn't have it back then when we were growing up. They didn't have it then, so, I think I am going with what I am, wrinkles and all. If you don't like it, oh well.

So, you are comfortable with who you are now?

Yes, there's not too much I can do about it. I'm just grateful to be here. I mean, I've seen so many of my friends, who have had real health problems, have died of cancer, that sort of thing. And back then, the treatments that they had for strokes when they were young women in their 50s... they didn't have the treatments that we have now. They didn't have the knowledge that we do now. I think that makes a difference at my age, because if I feel that something is not working right, I have no compunctions about calling the doctor and saying I'm having this or that problem. When I was younger, I wouldn't think twice about something that hurt. Now as I get older, I think I'm more conscious of what's working in my body and what might be a problem. If I have a problem with my feet I call the doctor. I'm not going to go get a pedicure if I should be going to a doctor. But that's just me.

Would you offer this advice to other women to take care of your own body and don't hesitate to call a doctor?

If you have insurance, which most of us do now in some form, it's crazy not to go to a doctor. I've seen friends of mine that let things linger and then things just get worse for them.

Is there anything you have done lately that made you feel young again?

I don't want to feel young again. It's taken me all this time to realize that I like who I am. I believe it's important to be who you are and remember who you were 20 years ago. Back then I wasn't as wise as I am now. I believe that.

Spirituality comes in all different shapes and sizes. Can you share how you approach spirituality during this phase of your life?

I was born and brought up Catholic, went to a Catholic school and was always involved with my church. Another thing that was instilled in me when I was younger was a need for prayer. I would tell my mother that I prayed to God to be able to do this or that and she said, "Well, don't be surprised if the answer is "no" because you're not doing it.

Which looking back was a very wise answer. All of us in my family have been involved in going to church and praying. I don't think that going to church had so much of an impression on me but rather what impressed me was my parents' belief in God. That faith came back to me in a lot of ways. For example, when my father had a stroke, I didn't question it. We all pitched in and did what we needed to help him and didn't question why. We just went on and I think that's part of my faith that has helped me today. You believe in what God is giving you for your life. I believe in the blessings. I believe in angels. I believe an angel is always on my shoulder even though I don't see the angel. I am very involved in my church and continue to do that to this day. I answer the phones, give vouchers for people in need of clothes or food, or electricity. I help them sign up for food banks so they can get food. I spend a lot of my free time helping at the church.

It sounds like you have given back your whole life.

I don't think I really gave back much when I was working because I just didn't have the time. I give back more now because it means more. When I was younger I had to work to survive. Now I volunteer and give back to those in need. I enjoy it because it makes a difference for so many people, and for me personally.

What kinds of things would you tell younger women about handling their finances?

Don't depend on anybody else to oversee your finances for you. I think that's key for women. My mother was great; she had great advice. You would love my mother. She'd be perfect for this interview. She sat all of us girls around the dining room table one night, after supper, my father was even sitting there, and she said, "Whatever you do in your life do not allow anyone to handle your finances whether you get married or not. You handle your own finances. After all, you are the one that has to pay for everyone."

She was a smart mother.

She was a woman ahead of her time. Let me tell you, I think a lot of that was the result of having a retarded child. She couldn't take him to a school since there weren't schools back then for kids like my brother. She took him everywhere and everyone in town loved him. They knew my brother because my mother always included my brother with the rest of us. My mother did not shut him away. I think that made a big difference in how my mother viewed life.

You have a positive view about money and finance.

Yes, because I have my own money and have worked hard for it. I've always taken care of my finances. I started working when I was in high school. I was washing dishes at a hospital seven nights a week and in the summer I was a playground instructor during the day.

Can you share anything with us that you do to keep your mind alert?

I read a lot. I read a lot of fiction but lately more non-fiction. As I said, my brother Tommy had Down syndrome and we found out that when Downs children reach or go beyond puberty they could get Alzheimer's. We didn't know that back then and we thought you could only get Alzheimer's when you got older. So as a result, I know a lot about Alzheimer's. Yeah, it happens to the best of us and I think because of that I read more practical things about health and welfare and look for things on what to do to keep my mind active. That is the most important thing, not only to keep your body active, but to keep your mind active. The mind is what commands everything else in your life. You know, whether you walk or you don't. Whether you get up or whether you sit down, you need your mind. I love puzzles. I do crosswords. I'm not very good at it, but I love them. It might take me a full week to do one crossword puzzle, but I try to do it without any help.

Can you think of any other activities that keep your mind healthy and alert?

Yes, I'm engaged in other things. I do a lot of volunteering at the senior center in addition to working at the church. I work in the office and also in the cafeteria. I helped them to establish a Cribbage group. No one really knew anything about Cribbage, so, I helped them learn how to play the game. Some other things that keep me active include doing word association kind of things. I used to love to read the paper and now we're paying two bucks for it. So I read it online, but even then it's not the same. I still like reading a real book. I like to be able to hold the book and turn pages. I go to the library all the time.

Some people say they have had difficult or stressful experiences but have learned important lessons from them. Do you believe that's true?

I think the most stressful experience was when my father had his stroke. That was four and a half years of stress, period. Then when my mother got sick, it took my father four and a half years to die, but for my mother it only took her three weeks. The stressful thing about all that, in addition to the grieving, was trying to determine what we were going to do with my retarded brother. He had always lived with my parents. That was stressful for me. I had to determine where my brother was going to live. My sister was a nun. We knew she was not going to take him. My older brother was married three times and was a bad alcoholic. My other sister was married with three kids and she couldn't take care of our brother. Then there was me. I had my own condo and was working 40 hours a week. He couldn't live alone, so I took him in. That was the most stressful time in my life I can remember. It was very difficult trying to explain to him about my mother's death, and why he had to come live with me.

So that was a big turning point in your life?

Yes, he lived with me for 11 years after my mother died. I was 57 when I took him in.

You're a saint to have done that. I don't think many people would have done that.

Well, I don't know about being a saint. Everybody loved him. He went everywhere and even now that he's been dead, people still come up to me and say, "How is Tommy?" I was downtown the other night and this couple came over to me and said, "We always remember you with your son." I said, *My son? He's my brother... he was 10 years older than me.* They were shocked when I told them that, but I think it's nice that even after all these years they still remember him. I carry that strength of caring for him during those days into my life now. It was difficult, but as a result I am a stronger woman today.

That's a great memory. What do you fear most about getting old?

I feel very grateful that I can get up in the morning. I don't fear aging because it's a natural progression. It doesn't scare me. When I was 30, I was afraid of getting old, but now I'm not. I'm not because I'm in a good place. I am on my own and I like where I am. I'm not perfect and I know it. I also know there are other things in my life that I could improve. As I shared, I am continually trying to do that now. I'm really enjoying every day. I might climb a hill or two here or there but mostly I coast for the most part. I enjoy life. I do. I really enjoy being who I am and being able to still do all the things I want.

Now that you know what it feels like to be in your 70s what advice would you tell someone that's younger, let's say in their 60s?

Just to be honest with yourself. If you don't feel good, seek help emotionally or physically. Keep friends close. Keep family closer.

Keep friends close, family closer?

Absolutely, because your family will always be there for you. I've known some people who don't have that association with their family and I feel bad for them. I know a couple of my friends, they haven't spoken to their brothers and sisters because of something with the sister-in-law or brother-in-law or whatever. I think it is really important to keep those avenues wide open when you get older. Stay true to yourself and keep your family close, if possible. Thank you for giving me the time this morning to share my story. I really enjoyed it.

DOES SHE OR DOESN'T SHE?

Yes, I am a blond. I believe all blonds growing up in the 60s and 70s were stereotyped as being Chrissy from the Three's Company sitcom. She certainly played her role well as a naive space cadet, blond bombshell type. Now that I am growing into my 60s and soon 70s I find when caught off guard or forgetful for a second, such as walking off the putting green with the flagstick in my hand, I laugh and say, "Guess I'm having a blond moment!" I quickly remind myself times have changed and my daughters would be outraged if they heard me say this. There isn't room for this kind of reduction for modern women in their lives today. So I only share my blond moments with my age appropriate woman friends and enjoy every second laughing at myself! It feels good to know where I come from.... the 60s and 70s which at the time, seemed to have an abundance of perfect television female role models!

Robbie (63)

THE GIFT THAT KEEPS ON GIVING

Ladies, here's the good news! I just found out that sex after menopause has some amazing benefits. According to the American Journal of Geriatric Psychiatry, having sex in old age improves your heart and mental fitness, improves sleep and can even boost your brain power. Here's the kicker. They found out that women who continue to have sex after 70 years of age perform greater on cognitive function tests than women who did not have sex very often. I am not surprised. That's probably why I am so good with Words with Friends!

Roberta (67)

❦

FUNNY GIRL

Laugh, laugh, laugh. Lucky for me I was born with a sense of humor. I can make anyone laugh, any day, any time. I love to laugh and even better, I like to see people laugh. It brings me great joy. As we grow older however, it can be difficult to find the humor in things we used to think were funny due to our aches and pains or whatever could be distracting us from life.

But look around you, there are a lot of funny things to laugh about. Watch some young children playing without having it bring a smile to your face-it can't happen. Laughing at our own mistakes are the best. Make fun of yourself; tell someone something you did recently that could bring a good laugh. One day I was in the grocery store waiting in line for the cashier to check me out. It was a very long line. Behind me stood this young man with only one item in his hand. Go ahead of me, I said. I'm retired and have time. You on the other hand look like you are in a hurry. "Thank you very much," he said with a smile on his face. As he moved to get ahead of the line, he waved to his wife, (who was apparently lurking in the background) to follow his lead and join him in line ahead of me. You know the next part… her grocery cart was filled to the brim. I was miffed at first, but then thought of the possibilities. I just laughed and thought, No good deed goes unpunished. I knew this event could someday make a funny story and bring a laugh to someone. I heard somewhere that laughing lowers blood pressure and can trigger the release of endorphin. I think laughing makes people feel better all over. I also saw this study in one of those senior citizen brochures that said older people who have a sense of humor live longer than those who rarely find the humor in life. I'm in it for the long run.

Barbara (69)

ॐ

THE WALKING DEAD

Just the other day I was at the library and noticed I was hungry but didn't want to leave for lunch. I decided to go to the coffee shop inside the library and purchase a snack to curb my hunger. Everything was expensive, so I decided on a small container of peanut butter pretzels. What stunned me about this entire interaction of purchasing these pretzels was not the outrageous $3.95 price for what seemed about 12 pretzels but the fact that the young woman waiting on me never looked at me. That's right, she looked down at the pretzels, said "$3.95", took my 5-dollar bill and gave me the change all without ever looking at me. The reason I mention this is that I have a little game I play when out in public. If I meet someone in passing or at an event and our eyes meet, I always give them a smile, and you know what? They always smile back. I've never had one person not smile back. This just makes my day. So when I met this young woman who couldn't or wouldn't look at me during what seemed like a two minute transaction, I was shocked and disappointed. All kinds of things went through my mind. I speculated all these cell phones and people walking around like zombies glued to an electronic device had something to do with it which is another conversation. Well anyways, one of my favorites sayings that I heard 45 years ago from one of my retiring employees is, "A day without smiling is like a day without sunshine." I have lived with that saying for decades because I believe it's true. For me, smiling makes me happy and even happier when the smile is returned.

Monica (81)

UP CLOSE and PERSONAL

Irene, Age 81

I arrive at Irene's home and enter noticing a bright, large Persian rug in the foyer. Irene is sitting in a comfortable chair with her leg in a black brace propped up on a hassock. There are two end tables on either side of her. These tables make it easy for Irene to retrieve her belongings. Placed upon the end tables are her iPhone, some books, iPad, pencil, glass of water, and eyeglasses. Irene slipped on her wooden floor four weeks prior to this interview, shattering her kneecap. At 81 years old, Irene has been told this could be a four to six-month rehab to get back to somewhat normal. Despite her injury, Irene looks regal. Behind her are ceiling to floor, glass, sliding doors. The sun shines strong behind Irene and lights up her blond hair and glowing skin. She is dressed comfortably, yet still fashionable under her circumstances. Her husband is there to greet me with an ice tea and a wonderful sense of humor. I challenge his humor with mine and then politely ask him to please leave us alone, to have some girl talk. He laughs sarcastically and turns to leave, but not without another funny, quick witted remark. He makes a point of telling me he hasn't left his wife's side since the accident.

I admire all the beautiful rugs in her home and let her know I appreciate their beauty and value. Irene immediately responds by letting me know these rugs were put back down on their floors after she slipped on the floor and injured her knee. She originally removed the rugs because she thought they made her home look dated. Had they been on the floor as they were for years, she laments, she may not be in this position of immobility. Irene is very positive and appears happy to entertain a visitor. At 81, her hair is lustrous with luminous shades of blonde. Her features are perfect even without makeup. I would never believe she is 81. I honestly would say she was perhaps 65. Irene is surrounded with photos of what seem like a profusion of grandchildren. She smiles and lets me know that her goal is to attend her granddaughter's wedding in California and not be in a wheelchair. Thank you, Irene, for sharing your time with me. I believe you will be at your granddaughter's wedding and perhaps maybe dance a step or two.

Can you share anything you did when you were younger you believe has contributed to your good health today?

First and foremost, I picked parents that lived healthy lives into their nineties, so I think genetics plays a big part. Also, I have never been a physical risk taker and I think that's important. I would never bungee jump or do anything like that. So, I think people that I know who were, let's say, more adventuresome than I was, some of these friends are not around today. Another thing that has helped me in my older years is that I never smoked. I rarely drink. I'm not adverse to it. I just don't drink much.

Anything else you can think of?

I've always physically taken care of myself, but honestly, I think genetics plays a big part in aging. My parents are both first generation Americans. My four grandparents were born in Sweden; I call it the good old fashioned Swedish peasant stock, sturdy people, very healthy. Also, I came from an unbelievably positive childhood. My childhood was absolutely as happy as it could be. I never had any adversity as a child which I think has made a difference in how I view life today. I was very lucky.

What about something you wish you hadn't done in your younger years you're paying for now?

Ooh. You know, what I often say at this point in my life, is I have no regrets. I married the person I wanted to. I did things in high school I wanted to do, but nothing major. I was with the popular kids, was head cheerleader all that stuff. That was important. Back then, I had the total support of my parents and got into the college of my choice. I was not the brightest in the class, but in a class of 180, I was in the top 25, which was good enough for me. I have no regrets.

Are there any activities you participate in that you feel contribute to the healthy lifestyle you lead today?

Well, I fell and right now I'm in a cast basically from my ankle to hip. I have never fallen in my life before. I was rushing around the kitchen, fell, and slipped; it had nothing to do with bones or aging. I was just heading out to play golf. Take out those six weeks that I've been in this state and I would say playing golf would be one. I'm not really athletic. That's why I was thrilled to be a cheerleader because we didn't have to take gym, so, I'm not an athletic person. I grew up with three girls in the family and we were not athletic. Playing golf keeps me active and I miss it.

Do you have any special advice for women to maintain their health as they grow older?

You have to take care of yourself on a continuous basis. You can't just say, oh, I think I will go on some special diet. You have to constantly eat as well as you can. Does that mean I haven't ever had a big Mac? Probably won't ever again, but yes, once in a while. But, really, self-care must be on a continuous basis. My doctor asked me about a year ago, "Would you like to live to be 100"? And I said, *Absolutely.* I would love to live as long as I was cognitively okay. I think you have to work at being healthy every day. For example, you have to go to bed at a fairly decent time because I read that as we age, getting enough sleep is critical; something about the cells in our body regenerating.

You mentioned your recent fall and the cast to your leg. How are you addressing this challenge?

It's just one leg. I've never ever been disabled in any sense before. I've never had anything go wrong with me. This is the first thing, and at 81 it's a shock, but it's healing perfectly. In fact, I went to the doctor and they are very happy with where my leg is at this point. The doctor said I'm at a very good place to be starting physical therapy. I think we heal better if we are in good health.

We know the downsides of aging and the changes that can occur in our appearance. Can you share how you are dealing with any of those changes?

Oh well, I sometimes think it's a shock to look in the mirror and say, *Hi Mom*. My mother lived into her nineties. It's a shock, because you're looking out of the eyes and mind you think is 36, and then you look in the mirror and say, *Oh my God. How did 81 happen?* You're going to have to begin to accept it, to accept things you can't change. Like, I would never do plastic surgery or anything like that, but changing the things you can change, those are good things. I try to walk, try to keep my diet healthy. I try to keep a good weight, keep my nails looking good, and have my hair done, those types of things. But I think it's important to do all the things you can do without doing stupid things, like going under the knife.

What about any advice for other women? What would you say to them?

First, you've got to accept the fact that you're getting older. Two friends of mine have Alzheimer's, and then another good friend died. I mean, this is hard at this age, losing friends. But you just have to accept you're getting older, embrace it and say basically, *Thank you Lord*. I do have one thing I'd like to share. This is going to sound corny. Every morning for a long time, I wake up, even with this leg problem, not being mobile, and I walk to the front door. I open the door and look up at the sky and I say, *Thank You Lord*. I am so grateful that I'm here. I'm 81 right now, not functioning the way I want to, but I'm thankful that I'm here and I don't take it lightly. I'm just unbelievably grateful I'm here. I also, which I don't like to talk about to anybody, have a very strong faith.

Thank you for sharing that. Another question; Can you describe a recent time in your life that made you feel beautiful and young again?

I'll tell you one thing. When I go to the doctor, for instance, with this leg, I will be sitting in the wheelchair waiting to go in and the nurse will call my name. I'll start to come, and she will say, "No, no, wait a minute." And then she will look at her papers and say, "What is your name? How old are you? When were you born?" I get a secret pleasure when I go to the doctor and the nurses say, "How old are you again?" Or when I was in the hospital and the nurses would disappear and walk in again and say, "I'm just checking to make sure that's who you are... you don't look 81." So that makes me feel good. It's a stupid little thing but you asked.

Let's talk about spiritual wealth. What spiritual areas, if you don't mind sharing, guide you through this phase of your life?

Well, as I said before I was brought up in a very Christian home. I questioned like everybody does when you're in college. I questioned everything and then I reformed my own faith, which is basically along the lines of my parents, but still my own. I go to church, not every Sunday, but we are considered part of the membership. It's just deep down inside, I have a faith. I know that my faith and my beliefs are with me, good and bad. I'm apt to say, *Thank you Lord for good things* as much as, *Oh dear Lord, how did this happen?* I had a grandfather who was unbelievably strong in his faith who said, "You never ever, ever stand on the street corner and practice your faith and spout out your faith... you just live it."

You said you go to church as your way to guide you spiritually. Is there anything else that keeps you in that spiritual, positive lifestyle?

You know what? I think some people are born more positive than others. I have an older sister who is a pessimist and I'm just the opposite. I'm not a Pollyanna, you know the type... everything is wonderful. I look on the bright side of things most of the time. I've seen it play out with this leg problem that I'm going through. It's been nine weeks I've been down, and I've been so aware of having to draw from my bootstraps. When you're going through it people call and ask, "How are you?" I would say, *I'm good, I'm really good.* And then I'd follow up with that I'm not always good, because I'm not going to pretend everything is good. But generally, I'm positive and I think that's really part of a person's personality traits. I'm making probably no sense right now.

No, no. This is making me feel good just listening to what you have to say.

Good, then can I add a little thing here? I believe entering each decade has its own challenges. I remember turning 30. When I turned 30 it was when everybody was talking about the Vietnam War and telling people "Don't trust anybody over 20". Oh my God, I'm 30. I can't be trusted anymore, I thought... thirty. I made it for Heaven Sake. So each decade you enter, it catches you up short. It really does. We are not thinking about what the next decade will hold for us.

Would you talk to me about the word wealth? When you hear that word what does it mean to you?

Oh my golly, wealth means a bundle. It means a whole box full. That box that is full of wealth, means health. I realized without health you have nothing. I believe wealth means family. It means friends. It means having somebody to love, one person, a husband. It means being financially secure, being able to do things that you want to do.

On another note, a lot of married women report that they like to keep a stash of cash available for themselves, just in case for whatever. Do you?

No, never. My mother did, but not me. There have been times in my life when my husband would come home from whatever business deal and say, "Here, this is for you" and I would put it aside. He knew about it and I could do with it what I wanted, but no, I've never kept money secretly. I am very frugal. So saving money is a big thing to me and it always has been. I always kept a little budget. I'm crazy that way. I drive my husband crazy.

Do you have any advice you'd like to share with other women about saving for their future?

I think women [my age] make a huge mistake. I don't think women do this today, but in the past, my generation did not take time to understand money; women have to. My mother made a comment which resonates with me today and I think is an interesting point. My grandmother was given a budget of 'x number of dollars' to spend each week or month. She would always overspend because she never knew how much money they had. My mother on the other hand, always managed the family money, so she always knew that she couldn't overspend. I've always managed our family money. My husband knows what we have, but I manage it so that in times past when we didn't have what we do today, I would say, *Well I can't buy that pair of shoes right now because there's no money.* He wasn't telling me I couldn't. I made the decision. So, I think women should know more about how to handle money. I think most women do today, but I could be wrong. It's a different time than in my era. Women were ignorant. You hear about women whose husbands die and they don't know where they're at financially. I think, are you kidding? I know every penny.

Do you think you pulled strength from doing that?

Oh my gosh! Yes, absolutely. That was a big part of different phases. I think women have phases in their life. I felt, at least in my generation, I preface everything with today. It's different. In my generation, you were in a certain socioeconomic group, went to high school, went to college and got married. You always had, as my mother would say, *something to fall back on in case everything went sour.* In my days, for a woman, that was being a nurse, a teacher or a secretary. So, I became a teacher, and my first phase in life was working in the schools. My second phase in life was being a mother, a housewife and a mother; this was the sixties and seventies. In this era the husband worked. My husband traveled all the time. He was never home. The kids say mom raised us. He was out doing his thing and was far more successful than we ever dreamt he would be. Our lives changed because of it.

My job was to take care of the children. I loved being a mother. I absolutely loved being a mother. Then one day, and this was a pivotal moment for me... I was shopping at the mall and said, *I need to hurry home and make dinner.* That's of another era too. Anyway, I said to myself, *wait a minute, you don't have anybody home.* I got myself a cup of coffee and I sat in the middle of the mall thinking. All right, your husband is running a corporation and coming home weekends. Your oldest son is in college out of state, and your twins have just gone to college. What are you hurrying home for? What are you going to do with the rest of your life? It was the most lightning bolt moment in my life. What are you going to do the rest of your life? I was in my fifties.

I sat there dumbstruck for a long time. I went home with the idea to ask my dad if I could work three days a week in his office. I didn't want to go back to teaching. I just didn't want to. So, I started working three days a week for my 81 year old father. He had trained a man to take over the company who didn't like that I was coming to help out with the business. He said to my father, "If she comes in three days a week, I will leave." So, another manager and I started delving into the books and found out he was stealing. We fired him and dad looked at me and said, "Do you want to run a business?" and because our name was over the door, I said, *Of course, Dad.* I would do anything for my dad. I ran his business for the next 18 years. Anyway, long story short, that was my next phase of life. I went from housewife, to teacher, to again housewife and then business. I take such silent pleasure out of what I did while working there.

That's a fascinating story. You mentioned about having a few friends with Alzheimer's. Can you share anything out of the ordinary you do to keep your mind thriving?

I don't know if it's out of the ordinary, but I try to read a lot. Oh, and I started playing bridge, which was unusual coming from a very strict religious family. I never held a card when I was young. We couldn't put cards on the table on Sundays. I mean, that's the kind of strict family I lived in. I decided I was going to learn to play bridge about six or seven years ago. Learning to play bridge was like going into a class that was spoken in German and not being able to understand German. Yes, I try to learn something new. I also try to communicate with friends, past friends and current friends. I learned how to use the computer. I can do a budget, which I have such fun with on my computer with QuickBooks. I just bought an iPad and laptop. I'm keeping up with the world of technology. It's helping me to keep my mind going.

What do you fear most about getting older and how do you address that fear?

The positive thing about getting older is you're still here. As long as your mind is good, realizing you do forget things once in a while, everything is still positive. I look at someone and I think, *what was his name? What was his name?* I hate that. What I do fear however would be the loss of control of your life as you get older. I've certainly experienced it more with this leg. All of a sudden I had to let my mind not get to that point of helplessness. Having this challenge has brought it to my attention more than ever before. I'm having to use a walker right now, although I'm not going to do that forever. I refused to learn how to use the crutches because I'm going from that walker, to the cane, to nothing. So I'm not using crutches. It's hard to think of yourself as old and marginalized and not right out there in front. I'm participating in life. I think it's hard when one feels marginalized and dependent and not participating.

Irene you're in your eighties and are so positive. What advice would you give women entering their seventies?

My friends are younger than I, all 10 years younger. Well for sure, I think it is critical to keep active to the best of your strength, your cognitive and physical strength. Keep active. Don't let little situations overtake you. You learn what's important and what's not important. Don't let little petty things get in your way. Sometimes I hear people complaining about certain things, and I want to say, *Get real. Are you kidding me?* Put everything in perspective of what is important. Is it important that your dinner wasn't cooked just the way you wanted or you had to wait an extra 20 minutes in the restaurant to be served? Is it important that you have a chance to talk with a friend? You haven't talked with them in a long time, so, keep things in perspective. Don't get bogged down on the silly things or the unimportant things. Thanks for this interview. I really enjoyed talking about some of these issues.

◐

DON'T LEAVE HOME WITHOUT IT

I am a consummate expert when it comes to bladder infections and tooth pain. And the older I get, the more I learn about these two debilitating show-stoppers. I love to travel and have cast the net wide since retiring. I remember, as if yesterday, the searing pain experienced in China from a murderous toothache that came out of nowhere and almost dropped me to my knees at the Great Wall. And I will never forget waking up in the middle of the night with excruciating and throbbing pain that felt like a bonfire taking off in my lower abdomen and not being able to pee. I like to call it the bladder infection from hell and almost lost the will to live. That bladder infection was pretty much all I remember about Barcelona, Spain. Have you ever tried to get antibiotics in the middle of the night in a foreign country? I don't think so. Or find a dentist to help with searing pain from an infected or dying tooth? Not going to happen. And don't think you are safe travelling in the United States. The middle of the night is the middle of the night. What I have learned and will share with other women in this book is this: I always, I mean always, have my physician write me a prescription for an antibiotic, and fill it before travelling in case I am forced to fight a bladder infection or toothache when travelling which I hear from others is quite common for older women. I'm not suggesting one ignore the doctor and self-medicate. Rather I am proposing one be prepared when travelling until you get home and can seek proper treatment. I now have my arsenal of pharmaceuticals with me to combat a bladder infection almost immediately. For toothaches, I pack an antibiotic and ibuprofen which both can work within six hours to stop the pain. If your physicians won't do this for you, sadly you might have the wrong doctor or dentist. It's a small thing to ask for, but I'd rather be safe than sorry. My doctors did not hesitate at all and both said I was wise to be prepared. Why ruin an entire vacation trying to find a dentist or spend time in an emergency room because you've been up all night with pain? Not me.

Rhonda (65)

A Day in the Life: Duchess, Age 70

5:30	Took dogs out for bathroom break
6:00	Took 20 minutes to engage in some stretching exercises
6:20	Caught up on some E-mails and did some University work.
7:20	Fed dogs breakfast and got dressed; Let dogs out again for second morning bathroom break.
7:45	Took one of two dogs I own to the Groomers; allowed the other dog to ride along.
8:00	At Groomers-long wait for service albeit no one was in front of me.
8:20	Arrived back home and ate my breakfast.
8:40	Took significant other who recently had back surgery for a barbershop haircut.
9:00	Walked other dog while waiting for hair cut to be completed.
9:40	Stopped by grocery store to get bananas on the way and newspaper for significant other.
9:50	Picked up dog from Groomers and brought him back home.
10:00	Climbed a tree to pull down an orange for dog. Took dogs out on a bathroom break
10:30	Participated in one-hour Zumba dance class
11:40	Ate a pre-planned yogurt snack with berries and nuts
12:00 Noon	Cleaned up kitchen from a meal last eve where the pots had to soak overnight
12:30	Face Timed with my seven year old granddaughter in Virginia

A DAY IN THE LIFE: Duchess, Age 70

1:00	Finished some personal items and checked on business ratings on several web sites to ascertain if I should invest with business; Ate lunch
1:30	Signed up for author's classes for children's books at UC extension and for a cooking class. Completed daily schedule for fitness, including a day for stretching, two days for dancing, one day for yoga, four days for dog walking, two days for upper body work.
2:00	Worked on Emcee agenda for Sunday for a President of a school leaving for another position.
3:00	Confirmed some student research information and coached a former student through some dilemmas
4:00	Called several people to confirm their speech honoring the retiring President.
5:30	Hoed up the orange tree's ground, deposited citrus fertilizer and watered.
6:00	Wrote letter of recommendation for a former student
7:00	Ate a snack; Looked at potential awards for my students in a Successories magazine.
7:30	Went food shopping.
8:30	Watched an Al Pacino movie.
10:00	Took dogs out for evening bathroom break.
10:30	Good night!

BOTCHED BOTOX

I don't think it looks that bad if I part my
hair on the right side.

❦

DOUBLE YOUR PLEASURE

I believe that if you are comfortable and things bring you comfort than why not double your comfort. I've always been a person who seeks comfort and classic when it comes to purchasing clothing. So if I love a pair of shoes that will be forever timeless and comfortable I will purchase a minimum of 2 pairs possibly 3! I just know they will be forever timeless and always a favorite! The same has always occurred with my cars! I have now owned 5 Volvo station wagons! Why? Because they are a dependable, classic safe car that has never let me down! Oh and they have a great service plan! Glasses and peepers are another multiple in my life! I can never have enough! Also lipsticks! I will keep a bowl near my entrance door to grab and go with my #450 Revlon! Never leave home without it! Flip flops and clogs in a basket at my entrance door are available for everyone to help themselves. In the winter I change to Ugh boots and slippers! Blankets, pillows and quilts are a must for everyone in my home to enjoy. I make sure that there are always enough for everyone's comfort. It's a New England thing...cold up here! Doubles or more are great if you believe in the satisfaction, comfort and practicality of the specific. I always love to please the people in my life and what better way than to shower them with double comfort and joy!

Peggy (63)

❧

RISKY BUSINESS

An activity that keeps me young is traveling and embarking on adventures that I ordinarily wouldn't have attempted. For instance, I recently zip-lined in Alaska and hired a helicopter to take an excursion to the top of Mendenhall Glacier. These two adventures reminded me how alive I am and how much I enjoy life as well as the beauty of the world around me.

Lisa (61)

❧

STEP AWAY FROM THE COMPUTER

I think it's important when you get older to make sure to leave the house every day. I don't watch a lot of television but am hooked on the damn computer surfing the web and viewing social media. One day I just said, "Enough is enough". I stepped away from the computer, got in my car and went to the mall. I did some window shopping and you know what happened next? I began to think of all these things I could do once I got home rather than sit at the computer surfing the net. At the mall I went into one of those cooking stores and saw some creative ways to make appetizers. I'm on it. I am now working at getting out of the house at least once a day and laying off the computer.

Marie (65)

❧

2 SIDES 2 MY STORY

My disabilities are a result of genetics and life experiences. Spinal disease and my consequent back surgeries were not directly caused by aging. I don't categorize my disabilities as "Age Specific". I simply know my limitations. Would I love to go Zip Lining or go on the scariest roller coasters? Hell YES! I know I can't due to a disability, not because of my age.

Deborah (66)

UP CLOSE and PERSONAL

June, Age 88

When I first connect up with June for our interview she is sitting in a plastic lawn chair at the edge of her garage, facing an alley that often substitutes for a quasi-driveway in many California coastal cities. Leashed to the lawn chair, her dog sits obediently at her feet. The temperature is close to 90 degrees and June is crocheting a wool cap for her grandson's birthday. Her iPhone is perched on the arm of the chair. The view through her garage is blocked with piles and piles of gardening items, furniture, jammed packed boxes of antiques and collectibles, and rows of canned goods stacked neatly on shelves lining the garage walls. Her new Jaguar perched in the middle of the garage, made me wonder how she manages to navigate to the main house without twisting sideways along the narrow aisle leading to her patio. I hear a humming sound coming from one corner of the garage and am alerted to an inexpensive box fan, working hard to provide air circulation. She notices my concern as I grimace over the fan crammed into such a compacted space smothered with stacks of magazines near its airshaft. She waves me back to her lawn chair somewhat annoyed. With a guilty tone in her voice, June shares she runs the fan day and night to keep the air flowing from the garage to her patio. I caution her, in my humble opinion, this situation is a huge fire hazard.

June lives alone with Bud, her rescue dog, in a small two-story townhouse she owns and once rented to her deceased twin brother. After her husband died she sold her large, coastal five-bedroom home for what I can only imagine was a small fortune. She said she misses her big house but confessed she likes living in a smaller place. The only thing wrong with living in this small townhouse, she complained was a lack of people to talk with like back in her old neighborhood. June is wearing a yellow sweatshirt, cuffed blue jeans, red lipstick, and a stylish, straw fedora. "Glad you wore a hat too," she says, reminding me that she always wears a hat to cover her hair loss. "And don't worry I hear you, I'll turn off the fan as soon as this interview is over."

Can you share anything you did when you were younger that has contributed to your good health today?

The only thing I've done that I think has helped today is that I knew enough to eat correctly and always got lots of exercise and moved around. When you're busy with three kids, you stay busy, and it's good for you.

How about something you wish you hadn't done in your younger years that you're paying for now?

I think I wish I hadn't been so nice to my son. He's not doing very much of anything with his life. I don't know, he seems happy right now. I guess that's the main thing I should consider. I began paying special attention to him from an early age. He was always special, and he was so cute. He was never a lot of trouble.

I hear that a lot from other women about their sons. So why do you think that is?

Well, in the first place, a lot of times there can be a certain amount of animosity between the husband and the son. We are always in the middle as mothers. We are always in the middle trying to protect the son from the husband. It's true, you know, and you're always right in the middle and you're either on one side or the other. Anyways, I was good to my son, but it took him much too long to finish college. I let him do that. I sent him to Europe. I did all the things that I could to make up for what I felt his dad fell short on.

Does that impact you now?

Well, not really. He's satisfied with what he is. He's got a great education. He will not use it. He will not accept authority. He prefers to live at a lesser scale than I ever would have been content with, but he's happy. I just think that if I had not been so nice to him when he was growing up, he would be more self-sufficient, that sort of thing. It's just now I worry about him after I am gone.

Can you describe any activities you're currently doing that influence your health today?

I continue to be very conscious about what I'm eating, what I put in my body. My mother was very health conscious. We ate correctly, and the food was always on the table correctly, the right food groups. I carried that on with my girls and for myself too.

So you follow that today? You eat good food?

Oh yes, absolutely. I have three meals a day. Don't tell me you can skip lunch or breakfast. Three meals a day were good then and more important now as we age.

Do you have any special advice for women regarding maintaining good health as they grow older?

Just keep active, keep running out there, get in your car, go and do whatever. Make your own fun. You don't have to have anything special. Sometimes that's all there is to it. Go somewhere every day.

Would you describe any barriers you're currently experiencing with your health and how you're addressing those challenges now?

Oh yippee. I sure can. I found a doctor that gave me a steroid injection and it absolutely took care of a six month limp and pain in my right hip. Oh, one good heroin injection, and I'm perfect.

Wasn't it cortisone? Did it hurt?

Yes cortisone, and no it didn't hurt one bit. I was limping around in pain for over six months, now I feel great. My advice for people who are experiencing some kind of pain is to tell your doctor about it. If you're old, who cares if you're getting a steroid injection? What difference does it make? You're not getting hung up on anything. You're trying to get comfortable.

We all know the downsides of aging. How do you deal with any changes occurring with your body or personal appearance?

I don't worry about it. Everybody earns their own wrinkles. A woman's job is to look as good as she can, as long as she can, but not be obsessive. I dye my hair so that I look a little less worn out. I believe you should put your lipstick on in the morning and look as good as you can when you go out the door. I'm fortunate because I can afford to do those things. There are many women who can't afford to get gas for their cars or get their hair done.

We all have a few special tricks to keep looking good. Could you share a few of them?

I use a vanishing cream every night and a good cleanser for my face. I'm perfectly happy with them. I use both morning and night.

Can you describe a recent time in your life that made you feel beautiful and young again?

Oh, sure. I took my dog to the 99-cent store the other day. While I was in the store a man came up to my cart. The man was maybe 65 years old. He admired my dog. "Oh, what a beautiful dog," he said. Then he looked up at me. I had a hat on, and he said, "And a beautiful Mama." I'm 88 years old. I don't care if I could smell alcohol on him... anybody that really tells me I am a nice pretty Mama, makes me happy.

What spiritual areas, if you don't mind sharing, guide you through this phase of your life?

I know that I'm going onto another and better life. I'm not afraid to go there. You have to do what you need to do here on earth, but God will take care of everything when the time comes.

Do you participate in any activities to maintain a spiritual balance at all?

No, I don't.

When you hear the word wealth, what does that mean to you? How would you define wealth?

Security, yes, security. I want to be secure, which I am.

What does that feel like to you?

Security feels like I am safe and will never be hungry or that I'll never be cold in November. I've been fortunate, and I do appreciate it, but I want to be secure and feel safe.

When we talk about money or finances, can you describe any strategies you use to keep up with the changing world of finance?

You have to keep yourself somewhat informed. Watch the stock market a little bit. Save regularly. I don't care what you do, but you must save a certain percentage or amount regularly. It doesn't have to be that much but just save. You may always have a sinking fund to worry about if you are investing in the stock market, but it's most important in the case of an emergency to have your assets built up. You cannot do that unless you start saving early and do it regularly.

Many women have what they call a secret stash of cash on hand. Think back to when you were married… did you ever have a secret stash?

Oh, yes, I always did. You can't trust anybody when it comes to money. Nobody else's values are exactly the same as yours. Back when I was married you knew that your husband could go out and bring home a new car without even asking or telling you. Be prepared for any kind of real crisis that occurs. If you really have to make him sit up and pay attention, you can say, *Well I am going away for a month or whatever.* You have to have assets to do those things in order to have power. I have done that. I've taken my children and said 'goodbye' until I felt it was healthy to return home.

What is the main thing you do right now to save money?

I save money when I grocery shop. It's fun. I have a good time with it. You read the papers to find out about the specials. There will be a day when newspapers have all the specials listed wherever I've lived. Here it's Tuesday. I'll go over all the specials and buy the fifty-cent Avocados. I love Avocados, but not if they cost me a dollar. I feel like saving money is a good thing when buying food.

Do you have any advice for women about saving money, spending money or whatever comes to mind?

You're responsible for yourself. You must take that responsibility as a woman. Nobody owes you anything.

What do you do to keep your mind going?

I read a lot. I like to read, which is fortunate.

Can you share an experience of something you've learned as a result of a stressful or difficult experience?

While my spouse was in the military, I spent many whole years alone with the kids until he got back from sea. One year, his brother decided to get a divorce and I had to take care of their three children and my three children. That taught me that I could work and take care of six children. That particular experience reaffirmed I could do anything. You can put your mind to anything if you really need to. I have lived by that ever since.

Looking back on when you were married, can you share what you believe is the secret to a happy relationship?

You have got to like each other. It's that simple. You've just got to like each other almost all the time. I did have a longstanding relationship after I was divorced where I thought he was the cat's meow and vice versa. That was the most pleasant period of my life. I didn't have to worry about whether I was uncertain about him or whether he would care if I asked him to do something. My spouse was difficult, so this relationship was different for me. This guy was a pleasure. Everything was easy. He thought I was a princess.

What do you do now for fun? What makes you happy?

I like to take my dog to the park. I take him twice a day. I try to go to different parks and talk with people who are walking their dogs. I have other friends I go out and grab a snack with. You know, nothing fancy, but hey, I get it, not everything has to be fancy. I get kick out of going to Del Taco as much as anywhere else. We have a good time.

What would you say are your major values or principles you live by?

I have to go back to security. I believe my values are knowing I am in a position to take care of my children should anything happen in the family. I'm lucky. Nothing terrible has happened. I appreciate knowing I am prepared.

What advice would you give to a woman a decade before you, someone now in their late seventies?

Women should be thinking about how prepared they are to be alone. They should have a certain amount of money to feel secure. If you need help you've got to be able to pay for it. Try to visualize what you might need as you get along in age. For example, right now I'm looking at different nursing homes so if anything goes wrong, I will know of a good place I would feel secure living in. You have to think ahead about getting older and not let things surprise you.

So be prepared. When did you start doing that, your whole life or just early on?

No, no, when I was about 65. When you start losing your parents you realize that the time is going to come when you better be ready to accept things changing or be prepared for new challenges you could be facing.

You live alone. The research says a large percent of women over 85 live alone. Do you ever fear living alone?

No, I love living alone. I can do what I want. I can eat what I want and when I want. I can get help if needed, if something breaks. For example, I have a regular cleaning service so I don't have to worry about cleaning my house.

Do you ever get lonely?

No, not particularly. I have three children who call me every night. My son comes to see me at least twice a week and my daughter visits once every couple of weeks and I can see my other daughter whenever I want. So, no, right now I am not lonely.

Thank you so much for taking the time to chat with me. Is there anything else you want to share?

I love books and I enjoy reading the kind of book you are preparing for women. I want to see how the others you are interviewing face the future. I suppose, some women are not always as lucky as I've been. I've worked hard, but I've been rewarded. I appreciate that I am able to be on my own at this age. For other women, make sure you get prepared for what is coming ahead as you grow older.

❧

WE'VE GOT YOUR BACK

Here is where all my BF girlfriends come to my side. Where would we all be without them? Our honest soulmates. I've always asked my girlfriends to be honest with me when it was in my best interest. Many have really reached out to me and helped me be a better person both physically and mentally. For instance I have woman friends who will let me know when I have that very visible black or long white chin hair visible that I did not pluck! Thank you friend! Or when I had a bad stain on the back of my pink leggings! Love you lady! Or when it's ok to cry because the son in law you thought you were close to having turned into a massive cheater and broke your daughter's heart! They were there for me supporting and kindly reminding me of all the things I can't see! I love my BF girlfriends! Thank you for taking care of me!

Rhonda (61)

❧

MORE NOVICANE PLEASE

I worked until I was 77 and could no longer keep up the pace of a busy dental office. After that I did some freelancing, but yes working until I couldn't physically do it anymore enabled me to purchase some real estate early in my early 70s that are now worth a fortune. Having that back up with the real estate makes me feel secure, that I can afford to move into a retirement home if I need to, that sort of thing. I found the older I got, the less money I needed since I just about ran out of stuff I wanted to buy; you know how that goes. So work as long as possible to stay young, that's my story and I'm sticking to it.

Evelyn (82)

A Day in the Life: Jessica, Age 61

8:00	Made coffee, got dressed, made bed and straightened areas of house, went through news, emails, Instagram, FB on iPhone.
10:30	Grocery shopped, went to T.J. Maxx for a planter, garden shop for herbs.
1:30	Unloaded car and then transplanted hydrangea plant my daughter gave me for Mother's Day.
2:00	Made an appetizer of blanched asparagus with a dipping sauce to bring to birthday party tonight.
2:30	Checked phone with emails, news and played bridge on app.
3:00	Made birthday present for girlfriend's birthday tonight which was putting together an herb garden.
4:00	Walked around golf course with pail and shovel collecting moss for planters on our deck, will plant tomorrow.
5:00	Showered and dressed for party.
6:00	Picked up the birthday girl and went to girl's night out at Barb's house.
6:30	Had lovely evening with The Jumping Jewels, close group of six women we all travel with occasionally...Barb made us lobster primavera, kale salad and paleo chocolate cake...Deb loved her herb garden.
10:00	Drove home as I surrendered to be the designated driver ☺
10:30	Went to bed and Ohhhh had a dream I was pregnant, and it was a nightmare! Didn't know who the father was...Yikes!!!

❦

DON'T HATE ME 'CAUSE I'M BEAUTIFUL

Getting older is an attitude. When someone compliments you on anything like, "You sure don't look your age!" just say thank you, look in the mirror and mentally agree. Let your attitude reflect you. You can be beautiful, sexy, vivacious, smart and talented at any age and remember with age comes wisdom so IMPART wisdom.

Sally (77)

❦

THE PAUSE THAT REFRESHES

Since turning 60 I am finding that things come at me much faster than ever. All sorts of changes are happening around me with my family, friends and society. Sometimes, I think I am becoming overwhelmed with the amount of information at my fingertips. My surroundings are for the most part positive but not always. There are a few changes that have brought me to a very anxious point in my life and as everyone knows, change can be frightening. I think, however, I've found a way to deal with my anxiousness and continue to survive these feelings. First I try and make my space as quiet as possible. Then I lie down on my bed and close my eyes and take myself to my safe place. I am still where nothing is coming at me nor do I send any thoughts or feelings outward. I am in a place where I don't go backwards or forwards. I stay in the moment and tell myself I am safe. It's as though everything is turned off and I only exist in my mind. It's a way to comfort and allow myself to be safe and secure. I've never meditated but sometimes I think this may be a bit like it. For me though this is my way of taking care of myself when no one else is around. It's my most peaceful place and I'm happy I can go there.

Polly (61)

GRANDMOTHER
IN WAITING

FLORIDA

༄

IS THERE A WOMAN DOCTOR IN THE HOUSE?

Many of us know women are better than men at doing a lot of things in life. I didn't think much about this difference between the sexes until I got sick and had to deal with a male doctor. Not only was he quick to put me on a brutal medication regime right away, but he wasn't particularly a very good listener. I tried to tell him I wanted to go slow with the treatment and work up to his suggested medication. He wouldn't have it. So what did I do? I went and found myself a female doctor who listened to me, seemed to care what I was saying and endorsed me starting out on a less aggressive treatment plan. End of story; it worked and I never had to take the initial recommended drug from the male doctor. One day I googled female physicians out of curiosity and read about a Harvard study done in 2016 that said patients who receive care from a female physician are more likely to survive and less likely to be readmitted to the hospital within 30 days of discharge (Harvard Edu. 2016 Hospitalized patients treated by female physicians show lower mortality, readmission rates). In fact they went on to say that 32,000 fewer people would die each year "if male physicians achieved the same outcomes as female physicians. " And there's more. There were pages upon pages of articles on the internet suggesting women physicians are better all-around for patient care. Hmmmmm… so glad I trusted my own instincts on this. My advice to women is seek out a female doctor if possible.

Jamie (69)

✲

BFFs

As far as being spiritual, I'm not a big fan of religion but I am close to all my children and their children which is very comforting in my older years. But the real spiritual feeling I get is from all of the woman friends I have made throughout my life and how many of us are still connected. Many have passed on for sure but my memories of the good times we had together is very import-ant to me in my life. Make a lot of woman friends.

Alma (89)

✲

POWER SHUFFLE

I used to run a mile every day, then had to tame it down to a power walk which I now call a power 'shuffle'. All the same my walk still works to keep my heart rate up and feeling good in the morning. In my younger years I made these runs a 'two-for-one' in that I would plan my day by making my to do list and, use the running time to solve immediate problems impacting me. About two years ago I read an interesting article about being present and decided to concentrate on doing just that on my walks. At first it was extremely difficult; the 'to do' list kept popping into my mind distracting me from my mission. It took a deliberate concentration to stay in the moment and look at my surround-ings, feel the wind on my face, and listen to the sounds all around me. I started to enjoy the feeling after a few days and came back from my walks more ener-gized and inspired than ever.

Just think, have you ever read a newspaper or book and suddenly realize that you can't remember what you were reading. You were actually engaged in the act of reading but your mind was preoccupied with other things such as prob-lems or having thoughts that overwhelm you with anxiety about the future. Living in the moment is not always easy. The key to learning to be present involves taking control of your thinking and squeezing out the internal conver-sations that jump into your mind.

Marilou (70)

UP CLOSE and PERSONAL

Rose, Age 88

I am excited to meet Rose since I'd heard so much about her from my good friend over the years. Rose is 88 and lives with her husband Larry, 99 years old. She is waiting for me at the front entrance as I walk up the sidewalk of her modest Huntington Beach home. The house had exquisite curb appeal showcasing a manicured lawn, trimmed shrubs and a newly painted entrance. Rose greets me at the door cautioning me not to trip, as she points to a step-down near the entrance. The inside of her house is immaculate and seems slightly empty. "Most of our stuff has been moved to my daughter's house," she explains.

I soon meet Larry, her husband of 70 years sitting in a recliner situated next to the dining room table. After Rose seats me at the table I am pretty sure Larry isn't planning to give us any privacy. "My doctor says once I turn 100, she wants to write a book about me," he shares as Rose sits down for the interview. "Now don't say anything," she cautions Larry, "she's going to turn on the tape recorder and we don't want you on it." Rose reminds me so much of her daughter, my friend, in looks, speech and strong assertive, demeanor. (LOL: Larry's comments were edited from this interview.)

I can tell by your demeanor and attitude that at 88 years old you are feeling pretty good. Can you talk about anything you did when you were younger that may have contributed to your good health today?

I don't really know how well my health is, but we've always lived a life without too much noise in it.

You mean like confusion?

No, not confusion. What I mean is that we didn't drink or live in excess, that sort of thing. We lived a quiet life. One thing, I smoked. I smoked very heavily and I'm feeling it now. I haven't smoked for 30 years. Thirty years later and I still feel the effects of smoking. I stopped 30 years ago, but still, with the weather when it gets humid, my breathing is affected.

Was there something you wish you hadn't done? It sounds like that was smoking.

Yes, I wish I hadn't smoked, but back then everyone did. Now, I'm living a quiet life. I have no extravagance or anything I can think of that would affect my health. I watch my diet very carefully and maintain a low sugar, low sodium diet to manage my diabetes.

Do you exercise?

My housework. That is my exercise. I clean my own house which keeps me active.

Do you have any special advice for women younger than you for maintaining their good health?

Yes, I would advise them to keep busy. As long as you keep busy and keep occupied, it keeps your mind occupied.

What kind of things do you do to keep your mind going?

Right now, I'm playing with my iPad that my daughter got me. I also do the crossword puzzles and I read as much as I can.

Are you experiencing any barriers with your health? You mentioned diabetes. How are you addressing those challenges?

I follow my diet and check my blood every morning to make sure it's at a stable place. I got diabetes about ten years ago. It runs in my family. My parents had diabetes.

Do you have to take insulin?

No, but I have to watch my diet. I can't eat whatever I want.

Can you describe how you feel about any changes in your body or appearance and share how you're dealing with those changes?

I just don't look in the mirror because that's what everybody says to do-just don't look in the mirror. At my age there's nothing you can do about it. You must accept it. I still shop for clothes when I can, and my daughter brings me new things to wear.

Do you have any special advice for women regarding their personal or physical appearance as they grow older?

Just be yourself and to try and act your age.

So, you don't even think about aging?

No, I don't think about it because you have to accept there's nothing you can do about it and dwelling on it isn't going to help anything.

When thinking about spiritual health, if you don't mind sharing, what kind of activities guide you through this phase of your life?

The same thing that guided us all through our lives. When we got married, my husband was Catholic and I was Jewish. We had grown up that way. His family was very religious and mine wasn't that religious, but we followed our faith. Today I follow my faith. He follows his faith. When we were married they thought it would only last six months because of our religious differences. It was considered a mortal sin to marry out of your religion. Imagine, we just celebrated our 70th anniversary. I think it worked.

Congratulations! Seventy years that's amazing.

Yes, we celebrated 70 years on Labor Day.

How old were you when you got married?

Eighteen. He was older than me.

I assume your parents probably put up a big fight about this marriage?

Yes. There was world war three.

When you hear the word wealth, what does that mean to you?

A person who is happy and healthy and has enough to get along is healthy, wealthy and wise. As far as I'm concerned, money does not bring happiness.

Did you always know that or was that something you came to as you got older?

No, I never knew that, but we lived that way our whole life.

Do you have any strategies about money you use now to keep up with finances?

My dad taught us when we were children that when you make a dollar, you should save a nickel. That's the strategy we've used and what's kept us above board.

You've always saved money?

We've always tried to save a little bit of whatever we had. We never lived beyond our means and we did not purchase things needlessly.

Many women I've interviewed say that they have always kept a secret stash of cash. Did you ever do that?

No. I never felt the need to.

Did you work when you were younger?

Yes, I was the publishing supervisor for GTE yellow pages for twenty-two years. I started as a clerk and then went all the way to the top. I retired in 1989 when I was about 59.

What is the main thing you do to save money at this stage of your life?

We stopped saving and now we give. We have five grandchildren and we have four great grandchildren. Grandpa thinks they must be taken care of when he's here. I don't know why, but that's the main reason for spending our money now and why we are not saving anymore.

Do you have any advice for women about saving money or spending money?

Just live within your means. Don't overspend.

We all know the fear a lot of us harbor as we get older such as dementia and Alzheimer's. Can you share anything you do to keep your mind thriving?

I play my games and do the puzzles and read. I do the crossword puzzles in the newspaper. They're getting a little harder to do at times. The Pilot brings me a puzzle every day. They're easier and I can really whip through them. I also play solitaire on the iPad.

Can you share any examples of a stressful time in your life that you believe had an impact on who you are today?

I don't know that I've had more stressful experiences than anyone else; there was nothing really stressful. I did have a stressful job though. Much of my responsibility was to manage people in a timely manner. I had many schedules that we needed to meet with the yellow pages. In addition to managing people at work, I was raising our family. I can handle stress very well now.

You've been married 70 years. What do you think is the secret to a happy marriage?

I always say marriage is a 50-50 situation. One partner gives 50 and the other one takes it.

That's a funny one. Any other tips? I mean, 70 years, my word. You could write a book just on that.

We've always communicated. We never did outlandish things. If there were some things that had to be discussed, we discussed them before we made any conclusion as to what would be done.

Do you still talk with one another a lot today?

We haven't talked too much this morning. It's pretty tough. But for some reason today he's pretty talkative.

What would you tell young women about getting married today?

They have to find somebody compatible. If not, it probably won't work out.

You knew right away that your husband was the one?

Yes, he was the one. He was right out of the service. Of course, he was 10 years older than I was, and he had a gold tooth. I thought it was beautiful. He hated it. He couldn't wait to get it out of his mouth, but at the time I thought it was really something. It just fascinated me when he smiled.

Were there any turning points in your life that put you on a different path?

Only going to work and advancing as I did. Having people with a lot more education than I who were working for me and having to take orders from me was a turning point. That situation lifted my self-esteem to some degree.

As a woman, it sounds like you were far along in your career?

Yes. And I didn't go further because I didn't want to move somewhere else.

Sounds like you could have moved up higher in the company but you didn't want to leave your home.

They offered me a job in Argentina to open the sales office there and I came home and my husband says, "You're crazy, they hate Americans."

So I went back the next day and my boss goes... *Well?* I told him I went home to my husband and as I walked through the door I had a rose through my teeth and he says, "No way, we're not going." So we didn't go. Then they wanted me to take over the office in Hawaii. And I thought, *Oh gee, that's super*. After much thought we decided to stay put.

These sound like the same issues women face today with their careers. It sounds like you had some leadership skills like your daughter.

Well I took leadership courses. I took a lot of courses working for the company. I started out part-time and moved up the company over the years.

What's the best thing you like doing right now at this stage of your life?

Playing with my great grandkids. There's nothing like it. Children are wonderful, grandchildren are wonderful, but great grandchildren, it's unbelievable.

What's so special about it?

Just even looking at them and thinking you started them. This is where they came from; me. It's a feeling that's indescribable. We have a seven-year-old, almost a five-year-old and two-year-old twins. That makes me the happiest of all, to be with my family

What do you most fear about getting older?

I don't think about it. I'm not afraid of going. They have a philosophy in my religion. They say that on this holiday that we're having now, Rosh Hashanah, that God opens his books and writes in the names of all the people who are going to live another year. Then on Yom Kippur, he closes the book. If my name is inscribed, I'll be here and if it's not I'm going home. It doesn't bother me. No, I don't fear it.

What are your major values you've lived by your whole life and continue throughout today?

My values. I love everybody. I have no bad feelings towards anyone. Be good to everybody. And treat everybody the way the golden rule is. Do unto others the way you want others to be good to you.

What makes you angry at this stage of your life?

False people. People who don't tell the truth always bothered me. That's the worst. If you're honest, then you have something that has to be said. Things can always be worked around. If you tried to get out of something by lying about it, that doesn't work. You're always found out anyway.

You mentioned on the phone that neither of you drive? When did that start?

I stopped about five or six years ago because I had neuropathy from the diabetes. I couldn't feel the pedals. My husband stopped this year in May.

What do you do to get around? You mentioned that you weren't going to go anywhere because your daughter was on a cruise.

We're not going anywhere. We arranged all our doctor visits before she left.

Do you know how to get a taxi or use Uber if you have to?

I know how to use Uber, but I haven't used it yet. You asked what scares me. That scares me. Getting into a car with someone I don't know would scare me. It's scary because you don't know what their motives are. A taxi is more legitimate probably because of where we grew up. In New York we held up our hand and waved down a taxi.

You mentioned you might live 50% of the time at your daughter's house and 50% here.

I'm not feeling too good about moving. I feel it's a burden on her. I would rather go into assisted living, but her father refuses to go into assisted living. He wants to live with our daughter. He feels we did it for my parents, she should do it for hers. We'll see.

Last question, what kind of advice, can you give other women about moving into their eighties?

Just keep active. Keep busy, keep active, and keep doing things to keep you happy. Oh, no, I forgot to ask you if you want a cup of coffee.

---

 cono

GOTCHA BIG BOY

After I retired, I kept my old sports car, a baby blue BMW Z3. It only has 70,000 miles and is in perfect mint condition; not a scratch on it. I've had it for over 15 years and for reasons I can't fully explain I can't part with it. Everyone tells me to sell it and get the new model. My husband even worries that it's so old it's unsafe. But I ignore the advice since this car has such good memories. I feel like I'm 20 years old again when I am behind the wheel. I always thought this car fits my personality and some of my friends even tell me they think it's my "signature car." There is one problem, however with this car. I have blond hair, fairly stylish, so when I'm driving and come to a stop light, the person in the adjacent car, mainly a man, will look over to see who's in the car expecting to see a gorgeous, young blond. When I turn around to take a peek, the guy quickly glances away, I suspect feeling a bit embarrassed. Luckily, I have great self-esteem and have a good laugh. This scenario happens every time, it never fails. Yes, I am getting old, but I can still turn heads ... sort of.

Mary (Age 69)

RISKY BUSINESS

Never Wear Socks When You are
Home Alone
ESPECIALLY WHILE TEXTING

❧

TAKE THE PLUNGE

For a long time my husband and I stopped having sex and it was the most ridiculous thing I could ever imagine. The good sex between the two of us was one of the main reasons we stayed together for so long. We were always good communicators when buying large purchases, raising our children; that sort of thing. But somewhere along the way we stopped talking about sex. My friend and I go out for lunch about once a month and she's always talking about all the great sex she's having with her new husband. I told her it was pretty dry at my house and she advised me to bring it up with my husband and try to find some solutions for our lack of intimacy. One night I did just that and the flood gates opened up. I won't bore you but that was the best advice anyone could have ever given me.

Marianne (70)

❧

RETIRED WITHOUT THE "RE"

The word I have removed from my vocabulary is retired. I look at a lot of people around my age who have retired and I say, "Thank you Jesus" for making me continue with life because I never want to look that old. Or be as 'tired' as people think we are! I never tell people I'm retired. When I think about the actual word "retire" it has such a negative connotations. When you look up the word in the dictionary it says, retreat, depart, and surrender. I want to think of my later years in life as being filled with possibilities rather than killing time with purple hair in an old folks home. Not me. I am not retired, I am reinventing myself every day!

Peggy (68)

A Day in the Life: Sandy, Age 67

4:00	Wake up, call of nature, have to pee. Lay awake trying to ignore the signal my bladder is sending to brain. Can I fall back to sleep without getting up? Stay awake until 5 and finally get up to pee.
7:30	Wake up, stay in bed thinking of day ahead. Do I have appointments today? Did I forget to go to an appointment earlier in the week? What day/date is it?
7:45	Get up, take daily meds, and rinse night mouth guard. Go downstairs.
8:00	TV on with morning news program. Discuss day's schedule with my husband, decide what to have for breakfast. Grind coffee beans, froth milk, eat and clean up. Check email.
9:30	Go for walk with neighbor.
11:00	Return from walk, take shower, put load of laundry in washing machine. Check email.
12:00 Noon	Goodness, time for lunch. Hubby goes out to lunch with buddies. I escape downstairs with lunch and watch episode of favorite program. The bliss of doing nothing and watching "Outlander".

A Day in the Life: Sandy, Age 67

1:00	Go to library to return/pick up books.
2:00	Knitting project sitting on floor, it's March and still working on last year's Xmas present for niece. Hmmm, should I knit or read? Reading wins.
4:00	Hubby home, "What's for dinner?" he asks. The usual conversation ensues....."I don't know. What would you like?" The discussion goes downhill from here.
5:00	Make pizza dough from scratch. Put in proofing oven to rise. Get ingredients ready for topping dough.
6:00	Put pizza in oven to bake.
6:20	Eat dinner, clean up, watch news.
8:00	Check email, play electronic round of mah jong.
9:30	Time to get ready for bed. Go upstairs, brush teeth, take meds, clean mouth night guard.
10:00	In bed with book. Hubby says don't stay up late reading. Tell myself to put down book at 11:00.
12:30	Oops, past my reading deadline...time to put out lights and go to sleep. Tomorrow is already here.

❦

PUT A YIDDLE ASS INTO IT

My advice for getting old… two words only, keep moving. When I was a dental hygienist I made sure that I did not sit down and that I was active in the office. My God the dentists I worked for all sat down on their stools and I can't name one that's still alive. So yes, I'd say be active and stay out of a seat. I am 88 years old now and have slowed down a bit but today I planted two tomato plants, walked my dog and plan to hose down the patio after my nap later this afternoon. Every inch of me hurts somewhere but what the heck, I'm not in a walker and I whole heartedly believe it's because I spent most of my life on my feet instead of my ass.

Peggy (88)

❦

😊 😊 😊

I often think about the joy I see on the faces of young children! The young children have a zest for everything they are experiencing. They are interested, they are engaged, they are confident, and they are happy! I remember how happy I was as a kid and wonder where that happiness went to as I grew into an adult. My goal now, in my sixty plus of age is to reignite that joyful spirt! In doing so, I will be able to continue learning and to turn frustration into fascination.

Carol (71)

UP CLOSE and PERSONAL

Mary Beth, Age 91

When asked to contribute to an interview for our book, Mary Beth, 91 insisted she come to my home. This was an opportunity to drive her car and get out of the house. Mary Beth is the mother of my friend Suzanne, who I've known for 25 years, which would make Mary Beth around 66 years old when I first met her. As I was getting ready to prepare soda, coffee and cookies to serve, I heard what sounded like two cars pulling up to my house. I thought it strange, two cars arriving at the same time, but looking out the window I saw Mary Beth driving a black Cadillac and my friend following behind in another car. Mary Beth is fiercely independent and loves to drive. She lives with Suzanne, her only child. From what I know they are inseparable, mostly caring for one another's needs.

Mary Beth is exquisitely dressed in pants, a sweater and two knit scarves draped over her neck and shoulders. It is 94 degrees outside. I am drawn to her bright, orange pocketbook laced with gold trim and her matching designer shoes. She has a beautiful blonde streak in her hair, wisping over her forehead. She's adorned with gold earrings, a necklace, and bracelet. Mary Beth gracefully holds her daughter's arm for support as she enters my home, checking out her immediate surroundings with a calculating look. She smells wonderful. As I wrap my arms around her, she calls me 'darling' and my heart melts. Mary Beth could be a movie star, she's that beautiful. I am flattered to know her and grateful she is giving me her time at the age of 91. I wonder what wisdom she will share with us.

I would like to start with the healthy part of aging. Could you share something you did when you were younger that has contributed to your good health today?

I think I would have to say good genes, good genes. I'm not really a healthy eater. I've been a strict vegetarian since the day I was born.

You don't eat any meat?

None whatsoever. I don't eat any meat and that's been from the day I was born.

You're from Ireland, how was that possible? Did your parents eat meat?

Everybody in my family ate meat. I'm one of seven children and everybody ate meat except me. I just couldn't eat meat. My mother said when I was little she'd mix it up with vegetables. I would put it in my mouth and then I'd pull the meat out. Isn't that weird? I don't know why. Funny enough, last night I saw on Tucker Carlson, there was a man on the show who said you can live much longer if you're a vegetarian.

Was there anything you did when you were younger you are paying for now?

I wasn't a smoker. I wasn't a drinker. So, I think I led a very healthy life.

How about activities you're presently doing you think may influence your health today?

For me, and I don't think anyone else would mention this, but it's driving. I love to drive. I think driving keeps me young.

I noticed you're not wearing any glasses.

I have glasses that I can wear. And once in a while I wear them, but I have been blessed with good eyesight.

And you've never had a problem getting the license?

No, not yet. I hope the next time they don't challenge me but if they do I will give them a good fight because I think I'm a good driver.

Do you have any advice for other women regarding their health as they grow older?

The greatest advice I could give them is to take good care of yourself. I think it's very important to take care of your body and groom yourself and not let yourself get overweight. As you know some people just don't care anymore when they get older. I would say just look after yourself.

Do you have any barriers you're currently experiencing with your health? If so how do those challenges impact your life today?

I've had cancer. I had breast cancer at 69. So, thank God I survived that. I had a heart attack at 88 and survived that. Those were my major illnesses. I am much stronger now. I'm doing fine and I'm very obedient. I do exactly what the doctors tell me to do.

Good for you. I'm sure your daughter is right there next to you.

Yes, my daughter is right beside me all the time.

Can you describe how you feel about any changes in your personal appearance or body and share thoughts about how you are dealing with those changes?

I have to tell you, I didn't ever notice any changes when I was 60, 70, but 80 was a big change.

In what way?

I got slower and I didn't seem to care as much.

Do you think something happened to you that made you feel that way?

No, not really, but I almost think I went to bed at 79 and woke up at age 80 and felt different. I don't think it was psychological. I just think

80 was a big number. Then when I hit 90, I didn't believe it. I still don't believe that I am 91 years old.

Do you feel different being 91 from age 81?

I do. I don't have the same energy. I don't have the same desire and everything's an effort. Being 91 is not easy.

You look beautiful.

Well, thank you darling.

For the record, you are exquisitely beautiful. People reading this should see the outfit you're wearing. You've even got a blonde streak in your hair in the front. You look awesome.

Well I do spend a lot of money on trying to look good. I think a woman's appearance is very important.

If you're not leaving home right away each day do you still get up and get dressed?

Every morning. I'm up at 7:30, but I don't get dressed right away. I have breakfast and then I watch television for a little while and then I get dressed. That's it. Then I go driving. I go driving every day.

What kind of car do you drive?

I drive my Cadillac.

Is it pink?

It's black. A funny little tidbit. My husband never liked Cadillacs and he used to say to me, "I don't like the people who drive a Cadillac." Little did he know, that when he died, I was planning to buy a Cadillac, which is exactly what I did. He did not like Cadillacs or Cadillac people. Isn't that funny?

It is funny. How long were you married?

Oh my goodness. When he died he was 52 or about 58. Wait a

minute now let me think... it was 30 some years ago. When my husband died, he was 58. Yes, that's it. He died of colon cancer at a young age.

Oh, that's too bad. Did you go and live with your daughter?

No, I lived in Spring Hill forever. Yes, until three years ago. Then I moved up here to live with my daughter because the doctor said I shouldn't be alone anymore.

Can you describe a recent time in your life that made you feel beautiful and young again?

Yes, I can. On Sundays I get dressed up and go into Boston. I have dinner with two of my granddaughters and sometimes even with their boyfriends. I always make an extra effort to look and feel good. It really helps. They all notice how I look and feel. They all love me. I feel a lot of love.

Oh good for you. That's important.

Yes, it's very important to be loved.

Let's talk a little bit about spiritual wealth. What spiritual areas do you attend to, if you don't mind sharing?

I'm a Roman Catholic. I'm not overly religious, but I do believe. I think everybody needs to believe in God. I pray.

Are there any other things you do on a regular basis to enrich your life?

I used to like to read, but my vision is not so good for reading much anymore.

What about church? Do you go to church?

Not anymore. I used to go until about a year ago, then I stopped going.

When you hear the word wealth, what does that mean to you?

Well initially? I think money but then when I dwell on it I know there are a lot more important things. I think having a good family and being close to them is being wealthy. I also think being there for them and to be loved. Oh no, I am starting to cry. I am not a crier.

You have a lot of love around you.

I've got everything to be thankful for. Everybody loves me, and I really know that the grandchildren love me.

When we talk about wealth related to financial capital, can you describe any strategies you used in your younger years to keep you financially stable?

Well my husband was a financial man and he did all the investments. I would say all my life I would hear, starting with my father, "If you have extra money, put it in the land. And you will not go wrong." I do believe that. I firmly believe that. I never knew anyone who put money in the land and lost it. They usually come out even or make money. So, that is one strategy. I would say put your money in the land.

Did you do that along the way?

We did. We always bought good houses in nice areas and it always paid off.

A lot of women report they have a secret stash of cash hidden away somewhere. Have you ever done that?

I wouldn't even think of having a secret stash of money. I only have the one child and she has everything I have. I'd like to tell you a funny thing about my mother. This might interest your readers. Being one of seven children, I had a brother Sam who was somewhat more wayward than the others. Not anything bad, but needier than the rest of us. He just didn't care as much. When my mother died she had this fur coat that was handed down to one of my sisters. My sister noticed the lining was a little different. Inside of the lining my mother had hidden some money in there for Sam.

You're kidding? Was it in an envelope with his name on it?

Yes, the envelope had his name on it and inside with the money was a letter that said, "*When I die this is to be given to Sam.*" She had a will and left money to people and everything, but this extra bit of money in the envelope was for Sam. Oh, isn't that funny, hidden in the lining of her fur coat?

Yes, very funny. Was it a lot of money?

Quite a bit of money. It was English money. It made a nice sum of money for Sam.

Do you have any advice for women as they age about wealth and money?

Well, I think I have given money to everybody, a little bit of money. I would say if you have money and can afford it, give it to people while you're alive so that you can see they get it right and put it to good use. If not, then leave it to them to do what they want. I believe in letting them enjoy it while I am here. That's my theory. Plenty of people don't feel that way. You still have to make sure you have enough money left to live yourself, you know?

What advice would you give young women like your granddaughters about personally caring for their own financial security?

I would tell them to not be ridiculous with their money, but to enjoy it and make a good salary. Enjoy it, but make sure they save some money. Put some away and save it. I don't believe in banking everything and not enjoying life. I think you should enjoy the money one has. To me, you can enjoy your life, or you can be miserable. I think it's important to do nice things, but still keep a nest egg.

Can you share anything you feel you're doing to keep your mind thriving?

Like I said earlier, I have good genes. It starts there I think and as far as I know, no one belonging to me ever had dementia or Alzheimer's. Then again, people could have died young, and I would not know it. I just don't have any strong advice for the mind other than to try to keep it active. Oh, yes, have friends. It's important to have good friends.

Do you play cards or anything like that?

I was going to and then I didn't. I should have kept the bridge up, but I didn't.

What about the computer

I can use the computer and a cell phone.

Do you feel comfortable with all the technical changes in the world?

I really don't have any trouble with that. Maybe it's because I'm active and I have the family around me. I think having family around you is very important. They keep me updated with all these new developments that are coming.

So you learn and listen to the children around you.

Yes, I do. I travel some. I used to travel a lot back in the day.

What kinds of things do you enjoy that are fun for you at 91?

I love Broadway and I prefer it. I love dramas. I don't like comedies at all, it's funny, I don't enjoy comedy, but I love a drama or a love story or a spy story.

You mentioned friends. What do you do with your friends?

Well, since I moved up here, I really don't have many friends. My daughter and her children and some of her friends are very nice to me, but I left my friends in Spring Hill. That was very hard for me. When I was with them we went to shows. We went to New York. My friend Jeanette and I traveled to London every New Year's Eve and spent New Year's Eve in the air. We always had a wonderful time, but neither one of us are fit to do that anymore. I couldn't do that now. I don't travel much anymore.

You're very alert.

Thank God I have an excellent memory; better than some people younger than me. I don't think it's anything I do. I think I'm just lucky.

What do you fear most about getting older and how do you address that fear?

Getting old and getting older. I don't like it. It's not easy. Getting older. It's pretty hard. I noticed I drop things easily. If I take the top off my face cream it will drop and then it's very hard to bend down and pick it up. I mean, there are a lot of little things in your day to day living that you think nothing of. When you get older a lot of them become challenges. I'm accepting that.

Do you have any fears about getting older?

I fear dying but I don't dwell on it.

Do you have any fear of not being able to go somewhere or get up and down the stairs?

Not now, but I think down the road it might get hard. At the moment, I can do the stairs. I think at 91, for me it's just live in the moment, rather than worry about next year.

Well that's good advice. What advice would you give women a decade before you, now that you know what 91 feels like?

I would tell her to take care of herself, look after herself, go to the beauty parlor, and keep your appearance up. I think keeping your appearance up is very important and being close to the family and having family members that care about you is critical. You know, it's just living day to day.

What about eating and exercise?

I eat, but I don't eat very much. I have a very bad appetite and I am not a good one for exercise. When I was younger I did a lot of running and I did horseback riding. I would ride horses in shows when I was a young girl. One time, I had my hair in two long braids with my riding outfit on. As I began the competition my hat fell off and I was disqualified because my hat fell off. My point is, that today it seems like every young person receives a trophy for participating. There are no disappointments in young people's lives. Everyone is treated the same. There are no winners or losers. I think children today need to know that life can have disappointments sometimes. Life is not always perfect.

That was interesting. Do you notice anything else different about the world today than when you were younger?

Yes, very much so. I don't think there's the same consideration and good manners in the world today that we had years ago.

You mentioned earlier you felt the world was very large when you were younger. What do you mean by that?

Yes, when I was younger we never knew much about the world. We knew about Ireland, the British Isles and we knew of Palestine, but I was a young girl. We didn't have Israel and all these other countries. So suddenly, to me, the world has become very small because we know about almost everywhere now.

Do you think that has a lot to do with all the technology available today?

Yes, and I'm not sure I approve of it, at all.

Do you feel an invasion of privacy?

Not necessarily. I just don't think the internet is as good for the brain as people think. I think for the brain's sake, it's much better to use your brain. The children must do every computation on the calculator, which for me, I can do in my head in a minute. Also, I think years ago everybody was much more polite. Today it's about getting it done right and people don't care about others as much. People are moving too fast and always looking at their phones.

Is there anything else you'd like to contribute?

I'm trying to think darling. Have I been of help today? Maybe I'm different than a lot of other women, you know. I consider myself very lucky.

Yes, you are lucky and fortunate and that's why I wanted to talk to you because there's a lot of women out there that can learn from what you said today. A lot of women don't know about other women your age. I have really enjoyed listening and learning from you.

Thank you, darling. It was a pleasure.

❦

CROSSING GUARD

Walking is something I do every day to keep myself fit and trim. I walk about 3-4 miles a day and cherish my time outside. HOWEVER, sometimes I think I am going to get killed walking. It's dangerous out there. As a pedestrian I sense my life is now in danger walking through crosswalks in a busy city. Just last week a young girl, obviously texting ran right through a stop sign and almost hit me head on. Earlier today a man in a pick-up truck, talking on his phone didn't see me in the crosswalk and came close to hitting me. I wear brightly colored clothing to alert drivers, but it doesn't seem to make a difference. Times are different now and people are not attending. I can't change the world but I can change where I walk. So now I drive to the park and walk on the strand. Oh no, yesterday someone was texting while walking and almost ran into me on the sidewalk. People. Put. Those. Phones. Down.

Gina (72)

❦

SHE WORKS HARD FOR THE MONEY

I am 70 years old and still working a full-time job. I have been a teacher, school principal, and then held my ultimate dream job given my intense interest in gender studies, school superintendent. I thought I had finally met all my goals in life when hired as the first woman superintendent for a large school district in Fresno County California. Knowing that over 80% of school superintendents in the United States were men I felt I had achieved a milestone personally and professionally serving as a role model for aspiring women leaders. I loved every minute of this high profile, intense job. I experienced the typical highs and lows of the profession but overall was successful as a women leader. I was also equally fortunate to retire at 62, a good time to exit the profession given the restrictions of the California retirement system. What I did not do that I could kick myself for was set in motion a plan for what to do after I retired. I would not recommend it. It didn't take me long however to set up a small consulting business and then write a book on education. But I missed the work; being connected to something bigger than me. I felt lucky a year later when I was hired as full-time professor for a university in their doctoral program. This opportunity for me was pure joy.

What I did not expect though was the response I received from friends and relatives. "What's wrong with you?" my younger sister chided. "You've worked your whole life, why aren't you taking time to 'smell the roses'?" she admonished. A close friend also scolded, "You're crazy. You've earned your down time, working at this age will kill you."

And finally, my husband, who was looking forward to some one-on-one quality time in our retirement was a bit disappointed to see me going back to work. He was however the only one in my inner circle who truly understood my motivations. Work, for me, WAS "smelling the roses". It always has been... working is what I love to do.

So why now, should I stop? I was, however, somewhat intimidated by the initial reactions from close friends and family. So in keeping with what I do when feeling out of synch with the rest of the world, I try to locate a new normal. I needed to discover what other women my age were doing after retirement. I was thrilled to learn that women over 65 were out there in the workforce in droves. And over 20% of women over 70 work full time jobs; the majority in professional areas, they did not want to leave after spending so much time on their education and skill building. Knowing these details gave me some comfort but I also had to back up my insecurities with women role models still working. The list was endless: Nancy Pelosi is 78, Jane Fonda-80; Gloria Steinin-84; Hillary Clinton-73; and of course, Ruth Bader Ginsberg at 85. Case closed. I am going to work as long as my health is good, until work stops being fun, or until I can no longer do the job effectively. At age 70 I'm still 'smelling the roses'.

Marilou (70)

So Claire. Don't you think they should put more wine in a bottle so there's enough for two people?

UP CLOSE and PERSONAL

Fannie and Gwen
Ages 100

We felt to complete our project on women and aging we needed to reach out to women 100 years or older. It was a challenge attempting to locate a woman who was able and without legal restrictions (willingly) to speak with us. One day, I mentioned to a friend that I was trying to find a woman 100+ years old to interview. She told me her mother was 101 but lived in Florida. Then she went on to say there may be someone at the nearby assisted living facility. So that was it! I immediately went to the facility and confirmed two interviews with Gwendolyn and Fannie. They were both 100! The perfect part was my sister was going to be visiting New England the following week and was able to coordinate her visit with the two interviews.

We walk into the assisted living facility each carrying a beautiful vase of festive fall flowers and are kindly greeted by the supervisor who is expecting us. Everyone is excited we are there to visit their two 100-year-old residents. When we end our interviews we all share hugs and pictures with our new friends. My sister will be back in California and I will continue to periodically visit with my new girlfriends, Gwendolyn and Fannie. On my next visit I will be delivering a lobster roll to one beauty of 100, and a box of chocolates to the other 100-year-old beauty. Thank you, ladies. You make our outlook on life that much more cherished.

Fannie Age 100

We are first announced to Fannie by the director of the assisted living facility. We enter her room and find her sitting in the corner near the window waiting for us. She is glowing. She is beautiful with Snow White wavy hair, a warm smile and wearing a soft blue sweater set embellished with flowers around the yoke. Fannie's walker is easily accessible in front of her. She is thrilled to have guests and loves her flowers. Around her room we glance at portraits of Fannie, husband, mother, father and an abundance of pictures with smiling children's faces. You can tell her faith is important to her as evidenced by several religious sayings and biblical pictures placed around her room. Fannie is so alert, friendly and very willing to participate in our project. We spend about 45 minutes talking with her. She never fatigues nor wants to stop talking. Funny, the staff warns us that Fannie loves to talk! For my sister and me it is an amazing moment on this day in October but for Fannie it is a 45-minute journey from 1918 to the present.

Fannie, thank you for meeting with us today. We would like to begin by asking you if you ever thought you were going to live to be 100?

Never, never. I never did because I had so many things that happened in my life that I could never think of living this long. Thank God I lived this long and I think I'm worthy of it. I appreciate everything that has happened to me up to these 100 years.

Can you think of anything in particular you did when you were younger or when you were in your sixties or seventies you believe helped you live this long?

Well, I worked in a school helping the teachers with kindergarten children. I loved children so much that I wanted to stay there forever. When I reached a certain age I couldn't do it anymore, so, I had to stop.

I stopped working, I believe, when I was about 70 years old. I didn't really stop after 70, however, because the children were gorgeous, and I enjoyed helping in a kindergarten class. That's when I volunteered.

So, you worked until you were 70?

Oh yes, I worked until I was 70, but then volunteered until I was 90.

What did you do from 70 to 90?

Well, I was going to kindergarten and helping with the children. I would read stories to them. I would play games with them. I would do so many things helping them in their work. I loved it. I loved every bit of it.

Do you think the working kept you going?

All the time.

That's what we're hearing from a lot of women.

I would look forward to it. So, then when I did have to stop working, I wanted to go back so badly, so, I filled in now and then. People would call me and ask can you help with this class or that class? I went into fifth grade a couple of times and read stories to the children. I loved it so much. I wanted to be near the children that I love best.

Your name is Fannie. How did you get that name?

When I was born my father named me after his mother, Vincenzo. Vincenzo is my real name. When my father would take us to school the teacher would ask, "What's your daughter's name?" Well, my father didn't know English, so he said Vincenzo, which is my real name. She couldn't understand Vincenzo so she named me Fannie and people started calling me Fannie. I said well, I'm sick and tired of just saying Vincenzo and Fannie. I went to court and I paid a dollar to get my real name, Fannie Maria and I was named Fannie ever since.

Do you have any advice for women about how to stay healthy as they grow old?

Well, I have been healthy for the most part of my life. I tried my best, but a lot of sickness came into my life as I got older and by the help of the Lord I am still here today. I would ask the Lord to help me when I would be sick with different things. I was at death's door three times and each time I made it. Every time something happened I would pray to the Lord, and the Lord helped me, and I came to. Here I am today to show you that God is still alive and waiting and helping people. So, yes, talk to God if you are on death's door.

Wonderful. What kind of health problems did you have?

I had cancer. I had breast cancer. I was also operated on for kidney cancer. The doctor said, "Well, we will wait and see what happens, Fannie." He didn't expect me to live.

How old were you then?

Oh, my, I can't remember. I was up in age some. I don't remember exactly, but anyway, I trusted God that he would help me. I believe God would help me. One day when the doctor came to check on me he said, "Fannie, it was the man upstairs that helped you." That's why I am here today.

We were wondering about all those pictures on your bulletin board. Are they your children?

No, these are the girls, 12-14 babies that I made the sweater sets for. I have made over 100 of them. When I was in Brooksby Village, that was another place, I would make these sweaters. Every time that somebody had a baby we would have a little party for them and the parents. I would make each baby a sweater.

Do you still make the sweaters?

I can't attend to my knitting anymore because my hand is bothering me, so, I had to stop. I made the bed spread right there that you are sitting on.

That's gorgeous.

I've made a lot of different things, blankets, and all different kinds of things. I even made a christening dress. It was the most beautiful one. I put it in the fair and I won first prize. The Christening dress was knitted with thread, with beautiful short sleeves, and with ribbon running through the waist.

You're beautiful. What have you done to stay so good looking throughout your life?

All the children made me that way. The children. I always looked forward to being with the children until I couldn't do it anymore. I believe 90. It was at 80 or 90, I don't recall. I did look forward to seeing the children. I also had to take care of my two sisters and a brother when they were children because Mom was a sick mother. She had a heart condition. That's why I had to stay out of school. I was 14 years old when they took me out of school. My Dad says, "You've got to come home and help my Mama." That's where I was until I grew up and met my husband, got married and had my own children. I have four children, two boys and two girls.

How long were you married?

Sixty-two years.

Can you tell us what the key is for a successful marriage?

Having children and taking care of my own children. My children made me happy.

You mentioned your husband passed away. How did you stay married to him for so long?

My husband became a minister and he had a little church. He preached in the church. He had shelves of books. We had to add a room in our house because he bought books and books and books. He was a grand reader. He was always looking up things to preach. He was a good man to be around because he knew so much about the world.

Do you listen to books on tape here or do you watch TV?

No, I don't. When I first got here I was sick. There was a lady in this room before me. She was one of the ladies that couldn't help herself. She was crippled, she was blind, and she couldn't help herself. Her mind was going and she talked a lot of nothing. She would keep me awake night and day, almost all of the time. They had to take her bed out of here because I couldn't sleep. That's why I didn't bother with the TV anymore. Now I could sleep.

You're very alert and you obviously know what day it is and what's happening around you. What kind of things do you do to keep your mind so alert?

Well, that's what I enjoy doing being alert. Knitting and crocheting helped.

Are you able to read?

Read? Well, I read the directions for all the knitting. I don't read much anymore.

Can you see fairly well?

Oh, yes, I see very well still.

You're 100 and everybody wants to live to 100. I know I do. Do you find any downsides to living to a 100?

Well, I don't feel 100. I don't feel like I am 100 because thank God I've got my mind and I can talk with people. I make things and talk about things. I just love the Lord and I want to help people if I could. So, that's what made me what I am today. I don't have any issues with being 100. My life is good.

You mentioned your brothers and sisters. Are they still alive?

The only two living are me and my brother. My brother's the baby of the family and I'm the oldest girl of the family. The rest of them are all gone.

How about your children?

I have four children. Two of them are still living.

Oh, wonderful. Do they come and see you?

When they can, but now they've moved out of state and I miss them so much. My brother, Sam, that's the one that's with me now, he has moved to Florida because his wife had what I have. She can't breathe well, so, they moved to Florida. These children are the only two I have living now. I see them periodically. They come and visit me. I can't travel too much anymore because of my walking and my breathing.

Do you have friends here?

Everybody here, they are all my friends. I love them all. I love people.

Fannie, is this a nice place to live?

Oh yes, I have friends here. I'm satisfied here. The only thing I don't care about is the food.

We would love to get some advice from you for younger women. When you hear the word wealth what does that word mean to you?

Well, wealth... I'd like to have more than what I have today. Not rich, but enough that I can get along. I'm not one of these that looks for riches. I was never taught that way at home because we were a poor family when I was born. I just always wanted enough to live on to be happy. I was happy with whatever I had until I had to stop doing the things I wanted to do because I couldn't do them anymore.

What about for young people? What would you tell young people today about money and wealth?

Wealth and happiness and a lot of money won't get you anywhere. It's with the help of the Lord that carries you through day by day. Without that, you can't do much of anything. Money will never get you any-where. You can live on it just naturally without saying, "Oh, I want that money. I want to make more money." Oh no, I didn't do that. No, I lived on what I had and what my family taught me when I was younger. Here I am today. I'm very happy.

What would you say you know now about living a happy and successful life that you didn't know when you were 30?

Well, let's see. I was married when I was 22 years old and I was happy with my husband for 62 years. We went places where we could afford to go because with four small children you couldn't take them too far. Once in a while we would have some nice relatives who would say, "Come on Fannie. Come and stay over three to four days and maybe even a week." I enjoyed going there. It was a change and I liked that. Outside of that, I was happy with what I had, and was satisfied. I wasn't always looking for bigger and better things. Now I live normally each day as I lived when I was younger.

Who was your favorite president that you can remember?

Oh, I had some nice ones, but I can't remember their names.

What do you think about the changes happening today with women? Do you think that women are coming into their own or do you think we have a long way to go still?

No, I think women are getting to the end now and it's not going to be too far away. Women have done a good job and I'm satisfied with what I see and hear. But some of these things that these men did to women that I am just hearing about is not good.

When you were born, women didn't have the right to vote. You were born in 1918, yes?

Yes, women weren't allowed to vote during that time. Now I know that I have a right to vote so that I can make things happen by voting in America.

Are you registered to vote?

Oh, yes. I've voted every year so far.

What do you fear most about getting older?

I don't fear it. I don't fear anything. I feel the same as I did 20 years ago when I think of my age. Thank God I'm here to live until that age. I've never been interested in how I felt. I just felt everyday things, you know. I could do as I wanted and go as far as I could. Like I said, so many years with kindergarten made me a happy girl.

What Kind of music do you like?

Church music. Not here though, because they sing the same songs over and over and I'm sick and tired of that. They ask me here, "Fannie are you going to come in and listen to some songs." and I say, *I don't want to since I've heard them over and over so many times.* You know, like "Let's go to the Ballgame" over and over. Where I lived when I was younger I used to hear people singing songs from my porch. When I came here I listened to a song once, or twice, three times, I said, *I don't want to listen anymore.*

Fannie, how long did you stay in your home by yourself before coming to an assisted living home?

Well, my husband died in 2000.

Almost 18 years ago? Did you live in a house together?

We had our own house. I did everything. I washed, I ironed and I scrubbed. I did all that stuff. When he died I had to leave.

When did you come here?

July, three years ago, I think. I've been here three years. Before here I lived in Brooksby Village. I had a nice little apartment there. Things weren't going right there and I was getting sick, real sick. I was dying. They put me on morphine every night to keep me quiet and sleeping. I couldn't hold food down. I was vomiting, and excuse me, moving my bowels every single day. I couldn't hold a drop of water and I was dying. Then my son said to me, "Mom, we've got to get you out of here because you're going to die." That's when he came and took me out of there. He brought me to another place in Danvers and I stayed there. They made me back to normal again and they gave me my weight back. I lost 10 pounds in one week and I gained all that back and more there. Then I came here.

Can you remember how old you were when your husband passed away?

Yes. When my kids got married and moved away; that's when I lived alone. And then things went downhill. You know what? I had to leave the house. I'd sold my house and I said, "Roger, I need a place to live if I have to get out of here." The people that wanted my apartment gave me one day to empty out full rooms and furniture. I lost everything. Everything. What I have is hanging in that closet. That's all I have to my name is right there in that small closet.

Who is that in the photograph?

That's my mum and dad. Also, do you see that puzzle on the wall? I made that. A thousand pieces. I put it all together.

Do you have any extra advice for women today?

Be faithful to your husband and your children and yourself and always do what your husband asks you to do. Follow his advice and you'll get along because that's what I did. I was good to my husband. My husband was good to me and then he got sick, cancer and it was gone.

Do you think about him today?

Constantly. Constantly. I close my eyes and I can see him. I would be thinking about what he would be doing. So many times he was working down in the basement, working in the garage and he would say, "Come on. I need some help. Hold this piece of wood." I enjoyed it because I loved him so much. I miss him so much. I still miss him. I close my eyes when I go to bed and I can visualize different things that happened with him in my life.

I have one last question. Are you a Red Sox fan? They are in the World Series today.

No, doesn't bother me. I don't care for baseball. I've had so much fun today. Thanks for coming here.

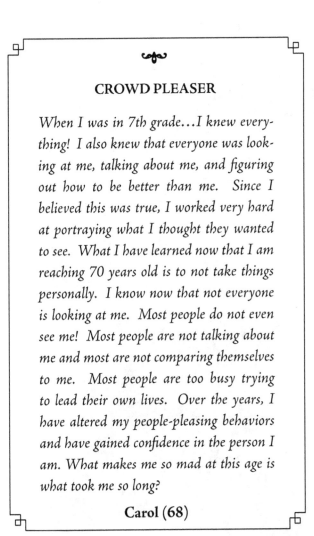

CROWD PLEASER

When I was in 7th grade…I knew everything! I also knew that everyone was looking at me, talking about me, and figuring out how to be better than me. Since I believed this was true, I worked very hard at portraying what I thought they wanted to see. What I have learned now that I am reaching 70 years old is to not take things personally. I know now that not everyone is looking at me. Most people do not even see me! Most people are not talking about me and most are not comparing themselves to me. Most people are too busy trying to lead their own lives. Over the years, I have altered my people-pleasing behaviors and have gained confidence in the person I am. What makes me so mad at this age is what took me so long?

Carol (68)

꿍

NBC HAS LEFT THE BUILDING

Okay, I almost hate to write this for your book about women and aging but I must. Watching too much TV can be the end of a happy life. I know many of us don't have a lot of things to fill our day but have you ever considered the downsides of watching too much TV? Just think… you are sitting and not being active. You are sitting there not burning calories and potentially adding to any weight issues. I don't know about you but when I watch TV, I eat lots of junk food. And what about the stress TV can generate? Sometimes after watching the news I can barely think straight. One day I added up the amount of TV I watched in one week and just about fell over. Monday-Friday I was watching 5 hours and then on the weekend up to 6 hours with football and movies for a whopping grand total of 37 hours. Yikes, that's well over a full day of watching TV. I knew I had to do something because 37 hours told me I was wasting my life. I made a rule for myself, which I am very good at, and said, No more than 2 hours a day. That's it… no more than 2 hours. Oh was that ever hard. The hardest part was finding something to fill up the remaining (37-14=23) hours I had to spare. Cutting down on TV felt almost like when I quit smoking; lots of nervous energy with nothing to do. Well, I read a ton of books, gardened, tried to bake some new recipes, and then signed up for a photography class at the Senior Center. I tried to find things to do that involved being engaged in something rather than passively sitting in front of the TV. It's been almost a year now and I feel so much better about my life. I have more friends, am happier, and think my mind is even sharper than ever. I can truthfully say, cutting down my TV time was one of the most challenging things I have done in a very long time. But I can also say gaining back (23 x 365) = 8,395 hours per year has been a real plus for me personally. Maybe next, I'll start on cutting back on my wine intake… nahhhhh!

Beverly (67)

꧁

PAGE TURNER

Read, read, read. I have always been a reader and I really think this is the reason why I can still pass the DMV written test today. People tell me I still have a good brain and that I'm not going senile... but how would I know if I was. I have read some type of a book every day of my life for as long as I can remember.

I can be in the 18th century in England one day and the next day on the streets of NYC... wonderful. Reading has been my little secret. I panicked a few months ago after having cataract surgery and everything was blurry for about a week. I thought I would die right there not being able to read. What a horrible life I thought, losing my books, but all turned out well and right now I am reading some nasty stuff on Trump. Television is okay but it doesn't draw you in like a book and actually I don't think it really helps keep the mind going... unless you are watching Michael Avenatti on the cable channels. Then I am engaged. Now that's a handsome fellow.

Janis (88)

Gwendolyn Age 100

Our next interview is down the hall to meet Gwendolyn. The staff informs us she likes to be called Gwen. We enter her room to find her lying on her side with her back to us. She was wearing navy blue slacks, a beige sweater and skid proof slipper socks. We are loudly introduced to her by the assistant who brings her lunch. Gwendolyn sits on the edge of her bed and starts to eat her lunch of chicken, vegetable and rice with sides of a grilled cheese sandwich and what we learn, her favorite, chocolate ice cream. At first Gwendolyn isn't sure who and why we are here. We wait in silence while she eats but then she says, "You can talk to me while I eat." We pull up our chairs real close because we want her to hear and see us. She tells us she is legally blind. We know right away she was hard of hearing. Several times she leans so far off the edge of her bed to hear us that we think she is going to fall onto the floor. We turn up our voices after a few scares. In her room we see three portraits; one of herself, her husband in his naval uniform and her mother. We also see a monthly calendar and a Christmas card with a dog thumbtacked to her bulletin board. We suspect Gwendolyn was a smart and spunky woman in her younger years who had a very witty sense of humor. Many of the things Gwendolyn shares lead us to believe she grew up an independent and self-sufficient woman.

Thank you for being with us today and allowing us to ask you some questions. We were excited to find someone who was 100 years old to talk with.

Really, it's hard to find someone that's 100?

Yes, it's very hard. You are rare. Gwen, can you share with us anything that you have done in your life to live to 100?

I was a school teacher so working helped.

How long did you work?

About 37 years.

What grade did you teach?

Second grade. I liked the little kids.

What did you do when you were growing up you think helped you live so long?

Everything.

Do you have any advice for young women today?

Just keep on living.

Did you think you were going to live to be 100?

I never thought about it. I just listened to everyone around me. Let it come whatever it is. Then I won't get disappointed.

Were you married?

Yes.

What's the key to a happy marriage?

A happy marriage?

Yes, what do you think a woman can do to have a happy marriage?

Well, I can't help you there because I didn't have a very happy marriage.

You didn't? Did you stay married?

Yes. Because I'm Catholic. But today? Today, I wouldn't. Today, I would say, *Take a hike!*

You stayed with him because you were Catholic, right?

Yes, that's right.

Why wasn't it happy?

He told me he wanted other women. I didn't think he was very nice and it was a difficult marriage.

You were a teacher. What did your husband do for a living?

He was a geologist. He was smart and very handsome.

Yes, because I see a picture.

That's me and that's him. He was the navy pilot.

You were a teacher. What advice could you give young woman today about money?

Hang onto your own money.

That's good advice. Did you have your own bank accounts? Did you keep your own money?

Yes, I did. That was important for me.

How many children did you have?

I don't have any children because I had a stillbirth early in my marriage.

Does anybody come and visit you here?

Oh, yes. I have two close friends who take me out. They take me out to lunch every once in a while.

Where did you go to college?

I got my first degree at Salem State. Then I got my master's degree at Boston University.

You did? How old were you when you got your master's degree?

Gee, I don't know. I think I went right from high school.

Did you pay for your own education or did your parents pay for it?

I paid for my own college.

Did you have any brothers or sisters?

No.

Then you were an only child?

Yes.

How long have you been here?

I have no idea.

Do you have a lot of friends here?

Yes, I have friends that come visit. I am going out tomorrow.

Where are you going tomorrow?

To Ipswich village.

Do you like the food here?

It's okay.

What do you do for fun every day? What makes you happy?

I play Bingo.

Do you win money and prizes?

Oh, yeah.

Do you play every day?

Yes, they have bingo every day.

When you look back at your whole life, what do you think was your greatest accomplishment?

Teaching school. I did it all my life. Kids liked me. Except for one kid, she called me a 'dirty double brat'.

Who is your favorite president?

Roosevelt was my favorite president. I liked him because he said, "A chicken in every pot."

Are you healthy now?

Yes.

Did you have any health challenges when you were in your sixties and seventies?

No health challenges, I sailed right through. Yes, I sailed right through.

So, you're a hundred years old.

I am the oldest one here. I'll be 101 February 25th.

Everybody wants to be 100. I want to live to be 100. Could you share with us any downsides of getting old and living to 100?

I don't have any. I just don't think about it. I feel fine.

Good. I see that you like ice cream. Is that your favorite thing to eat?

Yes, ice cream. Chocolate. I love chocolate ice cream. I like Treadmills.

Did you go there as a young girl?

Yeah. Loved it. I went there every night. It's still there I hear. I remember getting ice cream there.

What advice can you give to other women about getting old and who want to live to be 100 like you?

Just keep on living. Keep on living the best that you can.

Just keep living?

Yes, and stay positive. Do you think I'm positive?

Yes, you are very positive. What do you look forward to?

I look forward to playing bingo. I like that.

Do you sleep a lot during the day?

Nope. If I did that, I couldn't sleep at night. They give you a trazadone here at night.

Does everyone here get trazadone?

Yup, everybody. I have trouble sleeping and it helps.

Do you walk with this walker?

Yes.

You said you're going into the village tomorrow. How are you going to get there?

My friend is driving.

Are you going to the Village Restaurant tomorrow in Essex to get some fried clams?

Yes. I love fried clams.

I just love to ask people this. What was your favorite movie?

Gone with the Wind. I loved it when Rhett Butler said, "Frankly, Scarlett I don't give a damn."

You've been through a lot of generations of music. What was your favorite kind of music?

Classical. I used to play the piano for 21 years, and I played the violin for about 18.

Did you ever go to the Boston pops?

Yes, I remember that. I loved that.

Well, you know what Keith Lockhart is doing now? He's doing the music from the movie Psycho. That's his Halloween concert. He's doing it for two days.

Keith Lockhart? Yeah. I don't like Keith Lockhart. His marriage broke up.

Yes, you are right.

The violinist, he married the violinist.

How do you stay so sharp in your mind at this age?

I used to read a lot.

Do you watch television now?

I am legally blind. I can't watch TV or read books anymore. I can still see, but not as well as I would like to. You can't have everything in life.

Yes, you are correct. I'd like to ask you if you have any other advice for women today.

Yes, hang on to your money if you have it.

That's great advice. What about travel? Did you travel a lot in your life?

I have travelled a lot. I saw all the United States. Then I saw most of Europe, except for Japan and Russia. I didn't want to go there. I went with my husband. It was nice and I liked seeing the world. I'd never wanted to go to Japan because I remembered the war, you know, and all.

How old were you when you stopped driving?

I was 90. That was my freedom. I loved driving.

One last question. Are you a Red Sox fan?

Yes, I love the Red Sox.

You know they're in the World Series, right?

Yes. They're expected to win. Oh, I hope they do. I saw them when they won the last time.

Was that five years ago?

Yes, I saw them win. I thought it was wonderful. I was real excited. That was a big win. Yeah.

Well thank you very much for your time today with this interview. You have been wonderful, and we appreciate the time you gave us today and meeting you in person.

Thank you for visiting me today. This was fun. I hope the Red Sox win.

HOW TO PROGRAM YOUR NEW CAR
Carol's 45 minute training session with
19 year old Jason.

Carol tried to process all the technical information
the kind young man was telling her but all she could
think of was making dinner and hoping Jason would
just program her favorite radio stations.

SOME STILL LIKE IT HOT

I know I'm not the same woman I was when I was married at 27 but try to keep healthy and maintain a reasonable weight that fits my frame. Three years ago I was surprised by a vacation to Hawaii to celebrate our friend's 70th birthday. It was a return to our honeymoon destination 30 years ago! I was a tiny thing back then and a buyer for a large department store for the lingerie department. I had saved the beautiful wedding nightgowns I received as samples and wore on my honeymoon such as Christian Dior, Natori, Vanity Fair, Miss Elaine. They were still hanging in my closet. Did I dare try them on? The last time I remember wearing them was at Kapalua and Mana Lani on the islands of Maui and Hawaii in 1984! I did and they fit!!! I was so happy. They fit but I was a bit more wrinkled and a slight less perky than 30 years ago. So I hand washed them and packed them for our trip! Yes, I wore them once again on my return to Hawaii and felt as beautiful as I did when I was 27! I may not have been a bathing beauty in the eyes of the young honeymooners that were there at the time but in my husband's eyes I hadn't changed a bit since our honeymoon over 30 years ago!

Sarah (66)

❦

THE QUICKER PICKER UPPER

As I grew older I became less inspired about life in general with each passing day. Some days I would wake up in the morning and find myself feeling drained with absolutely nothing to do. I knew I could watch television, but I have a hard fast rule not to turn on the TV before 6:00 in the evening. I could read a book or clean the house but all of those things seemed like work. I guessed that some sort of depression was setting in and I hated those days. One day I googled "Get Inspired" and saw a whole list of things that people do to keep moving, do new things and feel alive. As a result I made a "Get Inspired" check off list which included things from Google (go to the gym, read a biography, play music loud in the house) and some that I thought up on my own (change routine for the day, take cell phone pictures and make a collage to send to my children). I even purchased a small white board and wrote down things I could consider in case I ever got in that state of mind again. So now if I wake up in the morning with that "do nothing stranded" feeling in the pit of my stomach, I make sure I check my Get Inspired Board.

Bella (74)

FINAL IMPRESSIONS

First and foremost, as sisters we had a lot of fun reconnecting while writing our book especially since we both live on separate coasts in the United States and rarely see one another. We never really felt as though we were distanced from each other, but this project was our transportation to reunite in the second half of our lives. We've had plenty of brainstorming moments but by far more laughs than anything. You must work hard to develop a friendship and we've accomplished that this past year. It's a wonderful feeling to have another best friend!

We both welcomed sound tips, secrets and advice from all the women we reached out to. These woman were truly Ambassadors of Aging. So much was shared that will help us all live healthy, happy and wise lives in the near decades.

We believe we have initiated a new adventure that will contribute to your own navigated journey. Whether you are 65, 75, 85, 95, or 100 you deserve to know you are much like everyone else your age. Technology has allowed us to look into so many embellished lives. We want you to know that even though we may think our lives are simple and plain we are very similar to one another. We are all coasting along attempting to achieve healthy, happy and wise lives. We all share the same ambition, to live to our fullest as long as possible.

Common denominators discovered were that most women we interviewed and talked to have a strong faith in God. In addition, most women shared that good genes make a significant difference in their health as they aged. Women had very few regrets while in their younger years growing up and the majority were pleased with their earlier lifestyle habits. All women, given a negative situation dealt with it and did not neglect their responsibility. We heard of many stories where women had serious illnesses or severe injuries. They all required great bravery and a positive outlook on life to survive. Many women attributed their strong faith or spiritual balance in life to a successful outcome.

As authors and interviewers we both had wonderful moments while engaging in conversations that were perhaps never revealed before. We always marveled at the trust and honesty exuded by each and every one of the women who participated in our book.

This book is a treasure and a tribute to all women over 60 years of age. That is why we will continue to share secrets and stories with all of you. We will be introducing you to more individual topics that will add humor and give you secrets and purpose for a better second half of your life. Ladies, we need your thoughts and suggestions on how to enhance and improve upon our life as we sail along. We would love to hear from all of you on our BLOG! We want to share how you are navigating your lives. We want to share your humorous moments, your successes and your beautiful moments of satisfaction living over 60! Join our blog and spend time with us! You can access and join our blog on our website at www.dontforgetyoursweatergirl.com.

Finally, this book has brought a sense of peace for both of us learning that women truly are in a circle of togetherness. We are bonded by the same existence of being born female. We've learned that our lives before 60 were extremely diverse. However, now as we enter uncharted territory we are connected more than ever before. We all desire a similar existence; one filled with family, friends, good health, happiness and an individual package of personal wealth. We want to live pain free and mindfully in the moment. We are all sisters through this journey. Why not do it together?

ص

MAKING A LIST AND CHECKING IT TWICE

Perhaps the most important thing reminding me to stay young-at-heart is making and referring to my bucket-list of five and ten year goals. For me, a bucket-list implies a sense of urgency to accomplish things I haven't yet accomplished before I die. This list includes not only places to travel and learning to quilt but also continuing to set educational goals that will allow me to keep my mind active and vibrant as well. As a former educator I remember telling my students, If it doesn't get written down, it won't get done. I really believe that. Just yesterday, I added learn to speak Spanish to my list! Lots of time and good things to do before I leave this world.

Gladys (68)

BEEN SHOPPING FOR YEARS AND
STILL HAVE NOTHING TO WEAR

CPSIA information can be obtained
at www.ICGtesting.com
Printed in the USA
FSHW010730210120
66312FS